A Safe place for Brent:

A Memoir about a Methamphetamine epidemic, a County Jail and a Community finding itself

By

Peter Denbo Haskins

www.theosisbooks.net

Cover Art by Joelle Paur

ISBN 9781070354552

Printed in the United States of America.

Dedication

To: Brent, who reached out for help and opened my eyes...all in the same motion.

Acknowledgements

The author would like to thank Fritz Pugh for his editing assistance with this project. His advice and work have been invaluable to making this book see the light of day. I want to say a special thanks to Ted for always believing in my projects and giving me the space to grow and create. His friendship is rare and eternal. Special thanks to my wife Emily who always has the time and patience to listen to my ideas. Her presence in my life is beyond precious. Special thanks to my son Dylan who gave me something higher to fight for than just my ego. He is an active source of energy, grace and joy in my life and for that I am eternally grateful and hopeful for the future of our beautiful and tragic species.

Contents

Foreword

My Community's Memoir

This is my memoir of my experience in Knox County, Indiana between 2005 and 2018. I founded and directed a drug rehabilitation ministry in the Knox County Jail called "Life after Meth" or LAM. I began this ministry while I was pastor of a small United Church of Christ congregation in Westphalia, Indiana in the northern part of Knox County. At the time I was a single Dad. I moved from Westphalia to nearby Vincennes to be closer to my six-year-old son Dylan as he began kindergarten. Vincennes is the county seat of government and home of the county's jail. I began working at LAM as my calling, as my ministry, as my social work, but I soon discovered that our entire community was involved in this mission. Why? Because the meth problem was *our* problem. Methamphetamine is a drug without a purpose. It's like an orphan, angry that it was abandoned at birth. It's vengeful and cynical and prone to lie and manipulate out of an innate sense of self-absorption. It takes no prisoners at the end of each battle. It exalts in this ruthlessness, the only power it really has.

Meth causes an immediate impact on an entire community, not just the addict and their family. I've seen this first-hand. We all have. The dirty syringes with their little orange caps which litter the street in front of my house are a testament to this ongoing impact.

9

I completely immersed myself in my adopted community, in the meantime healing wounds of being orphaned from my own roots, trying to feel connected, trying not to feel like a stranger. I felt disconnected from my community. I soon realized that most people around me felt this disconnect too. Little did I know the key to understanding this was contained within the walls of the local county jail.

Hearing a murmur

This memoir is really about discoveries. Everywhere I looked, I discovered something about our local criminal justice system, our community, about our country at large. I also discovered things about myself during that time working with the sick, those whom were tired, and disenfranchised. I discovered the people who inspired Jesus; the sick and the tired, the socially immobile and the economically sabotaged, the incoherent cries of the abused and the molested, the rage-filled rants at anyone who would listen. I heard these murmurs from the sidelines of society and those sounds came from one place: the county jail.

As the meth and drug problem increased in our community it had a wide-range of impacts. Some of them were obvious like public safety and homelessness. Other impacts were subtle. This subtleness I saw in the inmates who were released from the jail, even after just a brief stay in the jail. This issue was space. One of the most amazing reactions to someone who has experienced jail time is the issue of space. Every one of the men I picked up at the jail and took to the LAM House had a difficult time adjusting to the open space of the jail parking lot. They had been locked up for various amounts of time, some inmates spent up to four years at the Knox County Jail, and some just a few weeks. Nevertheless, they all had a difficult time adjusting to the sky above, the trees and the various moving objects, not to mention having a difficult time feeling calm even though they were free. In their mind, they were not free. Their physical captivity had actually altered their perception of space and these were the inmates who could move around an entire pod, not to mention the difficulty in adjustment by those who were held in any type of solitary confinement condition. Make no mistake, county jails have delegated space to accommodate 23/1 (23 hours in lock-down and 1 hour of recreation per 24 hour period) housing of troubled inmates as our county jails are America's new psychiatric wards.

This memoir is my story, the story of LAM. It is also the story of a community and what kind of impact addictions had and are still having on our community. This is really *our* story. In these past 10 plus years of doing this work I have several observations. One foundational observation: If you want to existentially understand what a community is about, look no further than the county jail. The county jail, *who is in it* and *who is NOT in it,* tells what you need to know about a community's history, its socio-economic priorities, its religious leanings, and its political beliefs. However, the jail also holds evidence of our country's wider system of social, political, and religious beliefs. We do not just live in a vacuum here in Knox County. We are impacted by social mores, national beliefs and political actions on behalf of our National Security which spillover into our corner of Indiana. Indeed, we are impacted by far-wider circumstances (many of us innocent victims) by political practices, economic cycles, and armed conflict. Most of these circumstances are completely out of our control. For 126 months I watched, I observed, and I listened and responded. I listened to the stories of the people who were not living the American Dream, they were the survivors, all orphaned in some way or another.

Every county in the United States of America has one: a local jail. It serves many purposes for the community. The county jail has many faces: it is a community's safety net, it's lent trap, it's garbage disposal, it's monastery, it's revival tent, it's pit of vipers, it's money pit and it's money tree, it's homeless shelter, it's mental hospital, it's triage unit. It is the depository of the ghosts and demons of forgotten faces belonging to hopeless families and long neglected neighborhoods who have died horribly isolated deaths. It is a testimony to a community's prejudices, its secret and proud racial bigotries, and economic injustices, which course through its veins like a wayward, vicious virus just waiting to awaken. In short, the county jail contains all the hope and dreams, nightmares and fever visions of a community as it stands at the crossroads with its past, with its aspirations and dreams and its subsequent failures and festering doubts and misgivings all visiting its present moment. Look no further than the mug shots at the jail (posted on various websites from our community radio stations): the bizarre faces of scolded children and wannabe criminals mixed with overwhelming fear and exhaustion on their mischievous and tattooed faces.

Whether sinister or not, our present dysfunctional criminal justice system is intentionally creating a new sub-group of poor and lower class citizens who are permanently wounded and therefore unable to function 'normally' in our society. They are members of society who can only function in a jail or prison. I met so many men and women who, after they were released desperately wanted to be back in jail or prison. At least then, they knew what to expect, they were included, they were survivors in an environment they understood. It is my belief that this system is encouraged by our nation's pseudo- war on drugs which only serves to perpetuate the problem by creating a nightmare web of psycho-social hurdles and hoops to jump over and through, all the while feeding a greedy web of pharmaceutical companies, prison-systems and courts and probation/parole departments. This 'war on drugs' is a social problem driven by economic greed designed to keep the downtrodden down. I am a grunt in this uniquely American Army. I saw how amazingly difficult it is to truly pull yourself out of this hole called addiction when it is coupled with significant jail time leading to economic slavery. Being incarcerated changes you, damages you, never to be the same. It alters who you are and it takes mighty efforts to recover, and begin anew. Mighty efforts indeed. Most never truly recover. Most communities never do either.

The county jail is where all of this lies, where violence and the injustices of a community meet face to face determining who really needs to be there and who does not, who had the money to bond-out and who doesn't and who really needs to be there because there is no safer, no warmer, no dryer place to be. The jail is the actual physical location where we place the mirror to our collective face and see who we really are and who we really are not. The county jail is the place where a community can ask the question: who are we?

In order to help communities, our society, and the world regain its strength, we must collectively reach into one of the lowest social places of all, the county jail to give a message of hope. Hope that offers those who are sick and tired of being sick and tired the tools they need to heal, return to their families and refresh, leading to starting a new life. It is by recognizing and treating this ignored sickness that we can begin to heal and regain our strength. Our world needs all of us to be healthy, not just the 1%.

I want to tell somebody about it. I think that is really why I have written this memoir. I need to confess it. So here it is. Through these pages you will get a glimpse of what I was honored to experience. More so, I discovered something about my community and my society and my world that is glorious, wonderful, sad, and tragic all at the same time. These are the secrets of ignored sicknesses, which plague us as a community. These are the secrets of systematic injustice which plague us as a nation. These are the secrets of personal demons which hunt each one us down in very specific ways. These are the stories behind the headlines of the "opioid crisis" or the "meth epidemic." There are real people behind these headlines and it's not always a nice and tidy plotline. Addiction ravages people and families and communities and nations. Whether we like it or not, we are all complicit. Whether we like it or not we're all on the same team. We're all Americans.

Introduction

A Stranger in a Strange Land

Call me a legal alien. Call me a stranger in my community, maybe even an social orphan. I have been living in Knox County since 2002. Nevertheless, I am a stranger, as I was not I born here. I was born somewhere else. Maybe I'm the only one who feels this way. Those born here considered me a stranger from another land. Although don't get me wrong, I am a white, middle-class, educated male living in the bible-belt of America, so I don't feel too sorry for myself. I have just never felt included.

Vincennes, Indiana is the county seat of Knox County, a town with a 2016 population of 17,924. The French founded Vincennes in 1732 as a fur-trading post. It later became home to Fort Sackville, a French outpost and settlement then most notably site of the pivotal military action led by Georges Rodgers Clark. It is one of the oldest and most historic cities in Indiana. Nestled in the southwest corner of Indiana along the storied Wabash River, it boasts as Indiana's first county, had its first newspaper, first bank, first University, first Masonic Lodge, first Catholic Church, first Presbyterian Church, and first medical society. I did not go to high school here; at Lincoln, North Knox, or South Knox, not even Rivet. I did not grow up in Vincennes; I am not from the 'Hill' nor the 'North End' nor the 'Bunker Hill' area. I did not play basketball in high school nor were my parents from any of the small towns, which dot the area. I have no understanding of the excitement in our community when Lincoln's Homecoming arrives every September and class reunions (mostly just opportunities for binge drinking) are held at every community hall in town. I have no particular affinity for watermelon, fudge, or Revolutionary War reenactment gatherings like 'The Rendezvous' held every Memorial Day weekend. I did not grow up watching the homespun comedy of Hollywood legend and hometown hero Red Skelton. I am aware of his paintings of frowning, sad clowns that are magnificently framed and hung on attorney office walls celebrating the heritage of this favorite son. I am a citizen and a participating member of my community but somehow I have never felt included.

Is it anyone's fault? Is it my fault for not trying harder...or my parent's fault for moving me and my sister around every four years...or my Scotch-Irish immigrant disposition living amongst the German gentry or the French Catholics? I am male, I am married with a family, and I am educated. I grew up living in the middle class in a United Methodist parsonage where we moved every four years so I have never really felt at home anywhere, always being on the outside looking in. I don't know...

I am an alien soul in the heart of this farming community nestled in the Wabash "Valley" of Southwestern Indiana. I am not from here and aware of that. However, I *should* feel at home since I am among the largest segment of the population according to the U.S. Census Bureau. According to genetic testing, I am 99.7% 'Northwestern European' in my own personal genetic test. I should feel right at home, but I do not. I am even among the 75% of Vincennes residents who were born in Indiana (having been born in Connersville in 1967). I should feel at home, but I do not. I try to intellectualize this feeling and I say 'none of us are from here... really. I mean we are all guests on this land really, aren't we?'

This community we call Knox County, it was once part of a vast swath of untouched forest, shared hunting ground between the Native American tribes of the north (*Iroquois, Miami, Ottawa*, etc.) and those of the South (*Cherokee, Chickasaw , Creek*, etc.) this vast forest was a buffer between the tribes. These rolling hills and vast floodplains near the Wabash River were once home to an enormous forest filled with wide-canopied Burr Oak, Tulip, and Maple trees teeming with life. Indiana really is beautiful country, once home to endless forests and wetlands and rolling savannas. In a wonderful 1997 essay published in *The Natural Heritage of Indiana,* Marion T. Jackson estimates that within Indiana's pre-settlement period there were 36,291 square miles of land, containing about twenty million acres of forestland, two million acres of prairie, and one and a half million acres of water and wetland with additional glades and barrens and savannas of another million acres. How I wonder what that land looked like...what it was like to be there in its pristine form? Knox County was a beautiful part of this land, hugging the southwestern corner where the White River and the Wabash met to flow down to the Ohio with its clear water. I feel home in the land that is gone, in the land that I will never see or experience. Why is this?

However, these primordial forests are long gone; either cut down for coal mining or cleared away for acres of feeder crops like corn and soybeans, as well as tarp-lined fields of seedless watermelon and cantaloupe. Man has been granted sovereignty over nature, right? We can do with it as we wish. The Wabash and White Rivers are now caramel-colored, drenched from industrial and farm run-off. Our Knox County community is seeded with the thoughts of this past with place names like *Piankashaw and Tecumseh and Quebache.* Our history is here whatever our heritage, whether it be Native American or manifest destiny, these influences are still among us, asleep in the soil beneath our feet. We live disconnected from our collective pasts. Yet we desperately seek to feel this connection with our past, to have an identity, any identity. Only the Native Americans are really from here, no matter what spin you put on it. We Europeans are interlopers and trespassers, connected only by place-names, jumbled and misinformed memories, fading and jaundiced and Facebooked into oblivion. I am an alien, a stranger, and by disconnection from my birthplace, an orphan like all of us here. We're all orphans.

17

There is little genuine pride in the land anymore. It has been co-opted by an attitude of selfishness and possessive arrogance. The land has been viewed as existing for us to exploit and use for profit and food and whatever else we choose to do with it. Our culture is disconnected from the Earth and it shows. We live on the land, arrogantly exploiting it until it is tired and emptied of its power and energy. We are a disconnected people. Disconnected from God? Disconnected from the land? Disconnected from each other? Disconnected from our very soul? Yea. All of it. But what can you do about it? This can only go on for so long, and then we must pay the price of our arrogance. My God, sometimes it all seems so clear to me. Our drug problem in America is a spiritual problem. We are cut-off from the source of our being. This seems so clear to me now...

Why did I start LAM?

I started LAM because addicts and alcoholics in my community were suffering and they weren't getting help. Plain and simple reason. As a Christian minister (let alone a Christian, period), I couldn't sit by and watch that happen. Suffering should be a call to action, not a thing to be pitied. I have every right to act in the face of pain and suffering and injustice and economic exploitation. Indeed I have a duty to act upon the leanings of my heart. We all do.

Personally speaking, my life has been so impacted, so transformed by my own relationship with God that I could not sit by and watch that suffering happen. God had gotten ahold of me and as the 20th Century mystic Charles Ashanin would say, "God entered my life and I cannot get rid of him!" I think that when God has truly awakened within your psyche, there is a natural outward progression. Religion is about 're-linking' with God. What does that mean? It's all about higher consciousness, this moving above and beyond our insect mind-set that we have been stuck in. It's all about higher consciousness. It must be. This is the unspoken connection between Paul's teaching and the teaching in the Letter of James (James 2:14-17). Faith without works is evidence that there was no initial awakening in the first place. Me? I had to *do* something in reaction to this awakening. Even though I had no idea what *to* do or how *to* do it, I chose to *do* in order to continue to *be.*

Throughout this book I hope you see what I have seen. That is what any writer really wants to do: share their vision, share their experience, share their world. One of the things I want to share is what I see in people in recovery from drug and alcohol addiction: hope. Once they get a hold of hope they will cling to it like a piece of floating driftwood after a shipwreck. Hope is all they have...hope in their future...hope in redemption...hope in a second, third or fourth chance with their daughter or their wife or their Dad...

LAM has introduced me to some of the most amazing people I have ever met in my entire life and I am going to share them with you. This book is full of instances and interviews I will share with you regarding these folks, these socially and economically deprived and spiritually malnourished saints who I now call my friends and allies. I will share with you some of their remarkable stories and some of my insights and hopefully, hopefully I will convey to you the excitement and the joy and the hope which can come from the true alchemy of ministry and social work.

Politics-free, 'higher-power' social work

Make no mistake about it, this is a book about ministry AND social work. It is not just for one or the other. It is for both groups. From my experience, I believe that the most effective drug rehabilitation programming is done when the faith community works hand-in-hand with the social work community, both of them utilizing their best tools to combat this crisis.

LAM is unashamedly a ministry which utilizes the 12 Step Recovery Program. According to Anne Fletcher in her 2013 publication titled "Inside Rehab," 80% of all drug rehabilitation programs utilizing the 12 Steps as their Evidence-Based Program (EBP). However there are a few vociferous disagreements from the social work side and the religious sides (both the red state and blue state sides) regarding the use of a program that even hints that religion should be a prerequisite at all and the other side that complains that the use of the term 'higher power' is an insult and a sign of an apostasy in light of the clear omnipotence and omnipresence of God, etc. [1]

In defense of the 12 Step Program (which I will talk about more as we move along in this book) I would say clearly that we utilize it as one of our essential tools in our toolbox because the 12 Steps are the nearest and best way at getting at 'conversion,' (which is the third and essential aspect of the program and the title of the third section of this book).

Let's pause and talk about this for a bit; my view of Christianity is that it is primarily a religion (the etymology of 'religion' means "to re-link") of *psychology* and not primarily a religion of *morality*. Christianity is indeed about living a moral life, yet you don't reach conversion by trying to be moral. [On the contrary, the fastest way to reach a life of high morality is by crashing and burning in a life of depravity and immorality.] Conversion is reached in other ways. In other words Christianity is not merely a learning exercise on how to imitate 'right, moral behavior' in order to insure your spot in heaven, like purchasing fire or earthquake insurance. Much of modern Christianity is just that: a club membership of people from a similar socio-economic and ethnic background. What a poor excuse for the church...the rest of the membership requirements are easy: just look and sound like everyone else...smile and pretend you don't have all that chaos going on in your mind with its racing thoughts about lust and greed and fear and anger and sexism and racism and xenophobia and jealousy and regret...forget all that, just keep smiling and pretend you are happy...it will all work out....Christ died for your sins and did all the work for you, right? Your job is to feel guilty and just accept his gift of new life...

I believe that Christ died for my sins, but I believe Christianity is more, much more than God's sacrifice and me being appreciative for God's sacrifice for me. Guilt doesn't lead us to a higher consciousness, on the contrary. I also believe in a psychological and physical work ethic that comes along with that sacrifice. Let's take a quick look at Scripture...in Luke 15: 11-32, Luke writes of Jesus telling the greatest short story of all time; the Parable of the Prodigal Son. It is the life of a recovering addict or alcoholic in a nutshell, amazingly perfect in its description of what this 'conversion' is like. In particular it describes hitting rock-bottom in a masterful way, stating in verses 14-17,

"When he had spent everything, a severe famine took place throughout the country, and he began to be in need. So he went and hired himself out to one of the citizens of that country, who sent him to his fields to feed the pigs. He would gladly have filled himself with the pods that the pigs were eating; and no one gave him anything. But when he came to himself he said, 'How many of my father's hired hands have bread enough to spare, but here I am dying of hunger!'"

This describes 'deflation' or 'hitting rock-bottom' perfectly. Perfectly.

I believe Christianity is just that, a 'coming to one's self' and realizing that you can't do it alone. The etymology of the word 'church' is after all "the gathering of those who are called out." You need God, you need friends and family, you need your community...but most importantly you need yourself. You need to find out who you are first, then all the rest will fall into place. And that is what Christianity is all about: self-discovery. This is what recovery from chemical addiction is about too. They are one and the same and the vast, vast majority of the people who inhabit this planet know nothing about this self-discovery stuff. Most people are as Henry David Thoreau said, "living lives of quiet desperation."

But for drug addicts and alcoholics who hit rock bottom and have a spiritual awakening, they know. It's funny because I have said many, many times at the Knox County Jail in our LAM groups and said, "Gentleman, most 'normal' people never get this opportunity in their life to reach toward self-discovery. You are the lucky ones." They look at me and shake their heads and say, 'That's all well and good Pete, but you get to go home at night. We are stuck here,' the inmates would say. I say, 'Yes, you are indeed stuck here...now figure *you* out and see what happens to your life and your outlook on your place on Earth. Stop complaining and get back to work on your resentment list on Step Four.'

Ironic that freedom would arrive in such a place: the county jail? Awesome irony!

There is a method to this awakening. This is the method of re-linking to God through the mind, through the psyche, through the re-training or the training of the mind. This is why prayer and meditation is such a missing link in the revival of modern Christianity. Bill W. and Dr. Bob understood connection with the mind and the importance of a recovery program which focuses on the thoughts of the alcoholic. One of the most effective types of chemical dependency programs in existence is the 12 Step Program. Why? Because it admits that addiction is a 'thinking problem,' not a moral problem. In my eyes Christianity is a religion based in human psychology and not morality. What a perfect fit.

Our LAM ministry was essentially about self-discovery, not only by the addict but self-discovery by the wife of the addict...by the son of the addict...by the aunt and uncle...the class-mate or neighbor...the arresting officer...the judge presiding at the initial hearing...the compassionate crossing-guard at Tecumseh-Harrison Elementary School when the addict was a kid growing up in the North End in Vincennes, Indiana. Recovery from any type of chemical dependency is a journey of self-discovery by everyone who is impacted by it, including the entire community itself. Addiction is essentially about suffering and suffering can be a doorway to a higher level of consciousness, either individual or collective.

If you can reach into the jail and work with those who are the sickest, the most broken...the most destitute and the most honest and the most abandoned then, *then* your community itself can begin to work on healing itself. By ministering to and helping their healing process then you actually begin to heal your community, the actual community itself.

This is not a moral issue

This healing can take years and years and years to occur, not just from the impact of the drugs and the years of alcohol, but from the years of physical, psychological and sexual abuse which these people have endured. If I have learned anything about drug addicts and alcoholics I have learned that this is not a moral issue! Chemical dependency is an issue of a disease, not morality. They are not addicts because they are bad people making bad choices. They are addicts because they have a disease. They have this disease because the vast majority of addicts are simply trying to survive. Survive what? They are trying to survive all the trauma which has occurred in their short life. Addiction for many, many addicts is actually just an attempt to hide, drown and escape all the psychological, physical and sexual pain they have undergone (primarily from this trauma in early childhood). I have heard story after story of abuse and neglect bordering on the diabolical done to children by their mother or father or cousin or foster-parent or pastor...all happening in some good and some bad neighborhoods but all of these happening in our collective community. This is why LAM heavily utilizes the 12 Step Program pioneered by Bill W. and Dr. Bob back in 1934; the 12 Steps are the most effective psychological tool I have seen to peel back these layers of abuse and pain. With the grace of their higher power and the help of other addicts they can eventually get to their real self, that self-actualization which Dr. Maslow talks about...that healed Gerasene Demoniac whom Christ healed...it's the same idea and the same act. The Steps guide you through this process of self-actualization, through this resurrection.

To no one's surprise not everyone LAM works with is healed 'in the twinkling of an eye.' Many negative, cynical people in our community look at those in our program who relapse as proof that it isn't working for anyone and *all* of these recovery programs are a grand, liberal waste of time. I believe that the opposite of faith is not disbelief, rather the opposite of faith is indeed cynicism.

Recovery from this disease take an incredible amount of effort and courage on the part of an addict as well as a community. It takes an amazing combination of circumstances to surround a person with the right sponsor, the right books, the right church, the right social worker, the right this and that...some people will never be at a place where they are willing to let their guard down and admit that their life is chaotic and that it has become absolutely unmanageable...some people will live their life on the installment plan, coming in and out of jail every few years until 10 or 20 years have passed them by and their life is a shambles. Yet LAM is not here to save every drug addict or alcoholic we meet. There will always be those who relapse and make the program look ineffective and useless, but what of it? We are here to work with those who are sick and tired of being sick and tired, not run a popularity contest or a political campaign. Recovery is not about perfection...it is about progress...and sometimes this progress is slow and awkward and bumpy.

...by healing our communities we can heal our nation...

And just think: what if several communities in Southwestern Indiana did this? What would happen if a whole bunch of communities across the Midwest did this...across our nation? Forget assistance from the Federal Government and Medicaid...let this be funded through local governments, mental health and substance abuse programs and faith community support. We might just find out a lot about ourselves as a nation and begin the healing process we need so desperately as we see more and more that we are riddled and baffled by our own violent, Civil War-driven past with its engrained history of discrimination and prejudice and stigmatization on a myriad of social and economic and religious levels. Growing-up in the Methodist parsonage I used to hear a lot about the potential our country has for spiritual awakenings, with three of them already in our history book as a nation in the 1790's with Jonathan Edwards, the 1840's and the latest pseudo-revival led by Billy Graham in the 1950's and 60's. I used to dream about that when I was in seminary: being a part of a great awakening of the Holy Spirit in America that would sweep through our nation and ignite the spark within our collective heart. When I was young I used to dream in red, white and blue, equating my religion with my patriotism. Since then I have grown and matured and no longer think that God is an American. I love my country dearly, that is why I ministered in our local, county jail with the section of our population who are 'disposable.' I think we revive are country by healing those who are sick, not locking them up and throwing away the key.

I see much of that thinking in the deep interest many Conservative Evangelicals have in this country's macro and micro political and judicial system, thinking that changing our country's legislation and legal composition will be the beginning of this fourth great awakening...but I don't see it this way. I am not drawn toward this kind of political expression of my faith in any way, whatsoever, yet I refuse to allow my own evangelical theology to be commandeered by a short-sighted if not well-meaning theology.

I am a 'Progressive Protestant Evangelical' who is deeply grounded in the theology and spirituality of ancient Eastern Orthodox Christianity but...I am also a 21st Century American who is aware of the need for relevant expression of this spirit of the early church in the church of today. Expression is key...and politics is not the expression we need to be using. To me, the way our country is revived and placed on any type of moral and spiritual foundation is ministering to one person at a time, helping them transform from the inside-out More importantly, it is about ministering to those who are considered the least of these. Jesus based his ministry on the lowest people in the Roman social strata. The 'modern' church has no idea what Jesus was really talking about when he talked about serving the poor and hungry and merciful first. I certainly had no idea until I worked in the county jail. Spiritual revival that has long-lasting cultural impact is created by making this message of spiritual transformation updated and relevant to our world. A spiritual revival is not manufactured through legislation and politics and secret dreams of power...but through ministry, real ministry of tending to the sick and the hungry strangers sitting in the prison...

Matthew writes, *"All the nations will be gathered before him, and he will separate people one from another as a shepherd separates the sheep from the goats, and he will put the sheep at his right hand and the goats at the left. Then the king will say to those at his right hand, 'Come, you that are blessed by my Father, inherit the kingdom prepared for you from the Foundation of the world;* **for I was hungry and you gave me food, I was thirsty and you gave me something to   drink I was a stranger and you welcomed me, I was naked and you gave me clothing, I was sick and you took care of me, I was in prison and you visited me.'"** (Matthew 25:31-36 NRSV)

The way we heal our country is by tending to the spiritually sick, abandoned and neglected in our society and come to find out...our country (literally) collects such people in our local jails.

Let me ask you this:

- Do you want a blueprint to heal your community from the ravages of addictions? If you said 'yes' then this book is for you.
- Are you an addict who is either sitting in jail reading this, bored and waiting for commissary or a can of chew or...are you a functioning alcoholic just sitting on your couch in the early morning, waiting for five p.m. to come so you can ride your son's BMX bike go down to the liquor store and buy a fifth of vodka... then this book is for you.
- Are you a family member who has a loved one or friend who is sickened by the tragic downward spiral you see happening before your eyes and you don't have any idea where to turn for help...then this book is for you.
- Or maybe you are just an interested citizen who has no connection with addictions in your life but you feel called to do something about this communal problem...then this book is for you.

The Vera Institute and Sheriff Steve Luce, Plantation or Jail, and Exploitation

I think there is a difference between knowledge and understanding. You can know something but not really have an understanding of it. Case in point: I knew that the county judicial system was a component and a driver in the increase of the prison population in the U.S., but I never fully understood the statistical and socio-economic importance until I discovered an amazing organization called the Vera Institute. They are headquartered in New York City with offices in Los Angeles, Washington D.C. and New Orleans. In a June 2017, report entitled *Out of Sight: the Growth of Jails in Rural America,* Jacob Kang-Brown and Ram Subramanian lay out the facts that America's 3,283 local jails are the "front door" to our mass incarceration problem. Yet for too long, county jails (in particular **rural county jails**) and the socio-economic problems that swirl around their communities have gone unnoticed. The Vera Institute reports that over the past decade the use of jails has *declined* in urban areas while it has grown even higher in *rural* areas. So much attention is placed on the urban areas that the problem in the rural areas goes unnoticed. 2

In the Presidential Election of 2016, we heard a clear cry for help from the rural areas of America. Knox County was no different. They desperately reached out to a populist businessperson who has chosen to take advantage of their fear and anger. Yet beyond the politics, the root causes of their cry for help are real and need to be heard and addressed. Christian Henrichson writes in the preface to the Vera Institute report,

> *Rural counties have been out of sight and out of mind in much of America. We saw this plainly in the last election. Their burgeoning jails are a window into the pain in those places, and a symptom of the challenges many of them confront-such as shrinking economies, deteriorating public health, negligible services, and pervasive addiction. In fact, the 2,623 primarily small and rural counties that chose Donald Trump in the 2016 election have more people in their jails and a higher incarceration rate than the 489 counties that preferred Hillary Clinton. 3*

Defined in the study, a Rural County is any county with fewer than 250,000 in population. Knox County having a 2015 population of 37,927 has seen an astronomical growth in its jail population. In general local jail populations have grown from 157,000 on any given day in 1970 to over

700,000 inmates in 2015, with nearly 11 million jail admissions in this country every year. Jails (not just prisons) are growing and growing quickly. Why?

One of the main reasons LAM exists at all is because of the former Sheriff Steve Luce's compassion, leadership, and vision. Steve Luce is one of those rare career law enforcement professionals who truly have a rare and admirable combination of personal loyalties. He is extremely proud of his time as Sheriff of Knox County. The safety of the community was extremely important to him. He also had a desire to live out his faith with compassion and equality while serving the citizens of his county. His creativity and excitement are to be given full credit in giving the LAM Ministry room to grow in the Knox County Jail. He saw the direction things were going in local law enforcement and was bold and brave enough to move in the direction of in-house drug rehabilitation within his county jail. In the end, he was a pioneer in this respect and needs to be given credit where it is due. He was elected in 2002 and then re-elected in 2006. He resigned in 2009 to become the Director of the Indiana Sheriff's Association in Indianapolis. In 2007, he and the Knox County Council decided to build a new jail as the old jail next to the county courthouse on 8th Street was desperately in need of renovation. Sheriff Luce invited my new organization (LAM) to start a program in the County's new jail and to begin to provide some drug rehab programming for the county inmates. At the time, the old jail was only big enough to house several dozen *local inmates,* however this new jail would be big enough (225 capacity) to house 'out of county' inmates which is potential revenue for the county. Not only was the old jail antiquated, it was completely (as was the community itself) unprepared to handle the sudden influx of newly formed and forming addicts as the meth 'epidemic' began to spread in the late 1990's and ballooning by the mid 2000's. What were they to do? They needed a new jail to handle all of the additional criminals and addicts, and they could even make some money doing. Jail rental: sounds like a good plan on several levels, right?

Come to find out, many, many rural counties across America were in similar situations. By 2013, the Vera Institute reports that 84% of all jails held some inmates (either pre-trial or sentenced) for other counties, state prisons, or federal authorities like Federal Marshals, Bureau of Prisons or Immigration and Customs Enforcement (ICE). Of the approximately 740,000 inmates on any given day housed in a jail somewhere in America, over 20% (approx. 160,000) of them are not under the jurisdiction of the jail they are housed. In addition, this sudden influx of new inmates in the rural jails not only caused a housing boom for jails, but also caused an enormous glut of people within these new jails who are *pretrial.* In other words, there was a sudden increase of what is called "pre-trial detention" where people are arrested and then they just sit in jail awaiting arraignment, trial, and sentencing. In fact, between 1970 and 2013 the rates of pre-trial detention have risen nationally by a whopping 436%. This means that over two-thirds of the U.S. jail population is comprised of people just sitting in jail waiting, just waiting. For those of you reading this book in jail right now, this problem sounds very familiar, does it not? This pre-trial incarceration rate grew most rapidly in America's 1,936 rural counties. 4

There are several reasons for this problem, which we have already referenced, namely the influx of new criminals and addicts in rural areas dues to local manufacturing of meth and the need to house them. This housing crisis could be solved or at least ameliorated by renting out jail space. The Vera Institute report explores one possible overall cause for this problem: "few resources in rural areas". They write, "Given that the distribution of scarce state and county resources is likely uneven- favoring those areas with more people-access to critical criminal justice and community services may be spread thin the further away a place is from the various population clusters in a state or county. This means there are fewer judges to quickly hear cases, less robust pretrial services, and fewer diversion programs available to decrease jail use."

Rural counties were inundated by a new drug, that almost overnight created an entirely new sub-group of addicts and criminals. The county attempted to meet this housing need and find a funding-stream for it…yet in the midst of this attempt created a glut of pre-trial inmates who had no adequate resources to meet their legal and addiction issues. According to the Vera Institute report, these rural counties need more judges, pre-trial services and a diversion program such as transitional housing…the LAM Program addresses two of these three problems.

Plantations to Prisons

On February 26, 2016, I heard an NPR report by Lynn Neary about a newly discovered prison memoir from 1858 by a black man named Austin Reed. The book is now titled *"The Life and Adventures of a Haunted Convict"*. It is comparable to other prison memoirs but is considered the earliest known prison memoir by an African-American. Mr. Reed was never a slave, but was sent to a farm at age six by his mother to serve as an indentured servant. At one point he was whipped for 'idleness' and subsequently set fire to a barn in retaliation for this whipping, as a slave would have been treated. Yet he was not a slave, indeed he had never been a slave. He was sent to The House of Refuge, the nation's first juvenile reformatory and later to New York's Auburn State Prison in 1840 when he was about 17 years old. While in prison, he learned to read and write, eventually producing this memoir in 1858. Reed's memoir was discovered in 2009 and eventually made it to Yale University where English Professor Caleb Smith connected Reed's memoir with other interpretations of the growth of the American prison system as a continuation of the Southern Plantation system and its systematic exploitation of slaves. Professor Smith points out that Reed saw the prison system as the inheritor of the plantation. Another Yale Professor named Robert Stepto, who helped edit and publish the memoir says, "Frederick

Douglas famously said all slaves are orphans. Austin Reed is telling a story of being orphaned, if you will."

As I sit and write my own memoir about my time working in a jail drug rehabilitation program, I realize how blessed I have been to have been born in the right family at the right time with the right skin color and the right education and the right whatever. I was able to leave the jail every day, go home to my family, and work on my own white guilt. It is 2018 and we are living in a time in America where the old storylines about America and race and the Civil War, which we apparently are continuing to fight, even to this very day. Politicians are exploiting the catch phrases and questioning our collective history and the very motivations and outcomes of that bloody war which caused 750,000 casualties and catapulted our nation toward the war on drugs which we are fighting today and which this memoir is so heavily based upon. This exploitation is based on fear and nostalgia and identity politics, which are all a very frightening combination. I am embarrassed for us as a nation that we have returned to these cruel and oppressive and dead ideas for guidance. It is proof that as Americans we are not as "Christian" as we thought we were. Nationalism and isolationism leave very little room for the God of Calvary.

Does society ever really get rid of the ghosts of their past? Are nations no different from people, unable to wash away the stench of the injustices and exploitations and systematic acts of cruelties by those in power upon those without power? It seems a revolving door on toxic memories that we cannot shake, the American people destined to relive the horrors of slavery, whether it be in a county jail or the NFL or the streets of Ferguson or Charlottsville. It seems as though we are hearing the same song, just in a different key...and no one notices. I saw this in the jail: the repetitive and hypocritical nature of how we exploit and manipulate a certain section of our population. The jail in Knox County contained the poorest of the poor in our community, Caucasian, African-American, Haitian and Latino. If you were stuck in jail, it was most likely a sign that you had no bail-money, plain and simple. Those who could afford the fees were able to bond-out, hire an attorney, and then litigate their case in court. However, if you were poor you were unable to afford bail, too often the only attorney available was a court appointed one. If you were poor, you were assigned a public defender who had caseloads exceeding normal capacities, you sat and waited for your turn in court, and agreed to a plea deal. In the modern American criminal justice system, the burden of guilt is placed on the defendant. The disenfranchised who are arrested have oftentimes already sealed their fate simply by being poor.

Exploitation

Nevertheless, who am I to talk? Did I exploit their suffering too? I mean, come on, for a decade I was able to sustain a career and earn a living from their 'bad luck.' Was my 'ministry' just a different form of exploitation? It is impossible for any clear-thinking individual to experience a decade in a local jail and not question the very nature of that facility and the system, which props it up when you see the same people enter the jail with the same socio-economic background, the same family names coming from the same neighborhoods and the same results. It is an inescapable question for me as to the nature of the fact that we have such a problem. No matter how one interprets the history and the current facts of our criminal justice and prison system, our collective history is not disconnected from itself. Our history is fraught with inequality, unfairness, and cruelty. An open-minded reading of that history is important in order to understand the nature of our problem. Am I saying our modern-day jails and prisons are modern-day plantations filled with modern-day slaves? No, I am not. Our jails and prisons are there for a reason and we will always need them. I am an advocate of and for our criminal justice and prison system in America. What I object to is the industrialization of our criminal justice and prison system in America and the subsequent exploitation of drug addicts and alcoholics in order to fill the beds in our embarrassingly large system of jails and prisons in America. In our typically Puritanical style, we Americans only act in extremes, having a very difficult time living in *moderation*. This proclivity for extremes runs through our American veins like black tar heroin and you see it in our religion, our politics, our drug use, our environment, and so many facets of our society. Drugs and alcohol contribute to the vast majority of all the arrests in America (anywhere from 85-90%). What I advocate for is that every jail in America has a robust and healthy drug rehabilitation program in place to try and sort-out these addicts from the criminals. That is all I am saying. Get in the jail so we can sort them out.

The Humanization of Addicts

What about these orphans from this war on drugs? Every county jail is full of these orphans, just waiting to be chosen by a new family. Every jail has inmates waiting for someone to come along and say, "You exist!" On so many levels they are a forgotten segment of our population, that collective amnesia by our communities is beginning to show itself. If you think about the statistics from the Center for Therapeutic Justice:

- 1/99 (2.3 million Americans) is incarcerated at this moment.
- 1/47 Americans is either incarcerated, on parole, probation, house arrest or housed in a local community corrections facility.
- 97% of all inmates will return home.

These numbers are staggering. Why? Because they are returning home, home to communities who are not prepared for their level of trauma and their level of un-employability. Our communities are simply not prepared to take care of this many people in a silent return to their 'old life.'

Many criminals sitting in jail right now are addicts masquerading as criminals. They are just addicts who never had a chance in life. Many inmates sitting in countless jail cells have had horrific childhoods. The case histories of individuals whose mothers abandoned them as children are heart wrenching. One particular story has stayed with me of an inmate whose mother abandoned him when he was about four years old. She left him and his 18-month-old brother to take care of them. He said he took care of his brother for a solid week, continuing to feed him with a bottle of rancid, spoiled baby formula. He and his brother survived but he became an addict. When I met him, he had been sitting in G-pod of the Jail for 9 months on check-deception charges linked to his drug use. His bond was $500 and he had no money and no friends or family to help get him out of jail. His court-appointed attorney had not been to see him in those 9 months. His story was amazingly common.

Another man told me the story of how his mother tried to drown him in their fish tank before she completely abandoned him. Another inmate tells the story of her mother leaving her when she was in third grade, completely on her own to take care of her younger sisters, in addition to finding food each day and getting them ready for school, doing homework, bathing. A young man remembers being abandoned by his mother when he was 9 and getting caught up in the Foster Care System. He tells the story of banging on the bathroom door trying to get to his Mom as she shot up dope with a strange man. She never let him in until she was finished...

The stories go on and on...poor and broke...abused and abandoned...the wrong last name...hearing voices or missing some I.Q. points...an inherited addiction or a chosen one, it's all the same result: abandonment, isolation and destruction. All aliens, strangers or orphans.

LAM and the Orphans

Life After Meth or LAM is a faith-based, not-for-profit drug rehabilitation ministry in Knox County, Indiana. Since May 1st, 2005, LAM's mission has been to create a new community of recovering addicts within our community. To create this community, LAM conducts a "Community Model/Therapeutic Model drug rehabilitation program" in the Knox County Jail for the volunteer male and female inmates. In addition to the jail program, LAM offers transitional housing to its male and female participants as a way to reconnect them (or in some instances connect them for the first time) with their children, their families, their jobs, their community and their God.

There are tons of jail programs in the country...there are tons of transitional housing programs in the country...but LAM was different, uniquely different and this is why: *LAM learned how to combine the best of Christian ministry and secular Social Work without losing the heart of either one.* In doing so, we created a faith-based jail program (utilizing the 12 Step Program) that was seamlessly connected to a sober-living environment any good Social Worker would be proud of...albeit this is nothing new, I believe that LAM was unique.

How was LAM unique? LAM was unique in that it combined the best characteristics of Christian ministry and Social Work without being bogged down in the trappings and arrogance of theology and dogma and medical models which can so often come with both ministry and social work. LAM not only assisted the addict in the early stages of their treatment with stabilization and rehabilitation in the jail, but also provided a safe place for the maintenance of their addiction in our transition houses. What is the key to all of this? The key is the establishment of sacred space within otherwise harsh environments.

Sacred Space

In 2012 and 2013 much of my spare time centered around a writing project which would eventually turn into a book published in 2014 by Theosis Books entitled *Seeking God in Violent Times: Religion in America and the Search for Sacred Space.* I was greatly impacted by my time in the jail and my realization of the importance of sacred space in the development of personality and community. Our churches are testimonies to this aspect. LAM's ministry was strategic in its focus on the development and maintenance of sacred space for the manner of *psychological* healing. Sacred space has two aspects to it: physical and psychological. Firstly, we create the *physical* sacred space within the jail, then within the LAM House, then within our collective community and larger, wider communities. Secondly, we create *psychological* space within the individual with the application of the (amazingly similar) 12 Step Program within the jail, at the LAM Houses and in our community.

It's all about establishing sacred space **within** the psyche of the human being first in order for our community to begin to get healthy again. In taking this person-by-person approach and working in the minutia of an addict's life, we see that our community begins to heal. It is the premise of this memoir that in order to heal a community, a family, a country the individuals must begin to heal first before any healing can take place. Isn't this what social work attempts to do? Isn't this what ministry attempts to do? We work with people on their level and attempt to give them room to heal, grow and flourish as human beings.

The LAM ministry was all about helping people find their way out of the hellish and demonic existence of chemical addiction and into a life of wholeness, harmony and radiance, as Thomas Aquinas would say about the definition of a piece of art. I believe that life is an art as well, each member of the human race being their own artist, forming and sculpting their life so that they have this wholeness, harmony and radiance about them. This is what we do at LAM, we help people (who happen to be addicts and alcoholics) become who they were meant to be, over and above just mere existence...LAM is interested in helping the addict find their purpose and destiny in life, their human transcendence.

Why?

Because transcending the limitations of human existence is one of the chief reasons people use drugs in the first place. Believe it or not, the vast majority of drug addicts I have served with are not bad, immoral people who are just too lazy, self-centered, stupid or ignorant to function in life. Many drug addicts and alcoholics I have worked with are really seeking something higher, something higher in their existence. They are seeking a way out, a way of escape. Drugs and alcohol were chosen as their guide out of this maze of anarchy they inherited (oftentimes at birth) and in that choice they made a tragic mistake. In this desperate search for escape from the abuse, pain and abandonment which accompanies this human existence they got stuck...they got stuck in that search...trapped if you will in the confines of their physical body, they got trapped within the memories and scars and tears of the abuses and tragedies and abandonments which they have experienced and have survived. They got trapped.

Now don't get the wrong picture. I am not advocating that every drug addict and alcoholic is a saint waiting in the wings, waiting to fly toward God. The people populating the ranks of addicts are no different from any other group of people...there are the good and bad and the ugly...and although not from the angle of a jail guard or a Sheriff's Deputy, I have seen examples of all. But that is not what I mean. We will always need jails and prison as they serve as a safety valve for our society as we constantly attempt to stave-off anarchy and chaos. There are many, many inmates who need to be in jail and prison (some of them permanently) and it is this class of felon which I am not interested in ministering to. I will gladly be labeled as 'mean' by some Christians (as I recall being labeled one time by a conservative Christian in our community), but I would counter that they are embarrassingly naïve if they think that everyone can be saved by will-power alone (of either the minister or the ministered-to). Salvation is God's business, not mine. I am trying to work in people's lives without placing undue expectations upon them. (It is amazing how much ministry can really just be a huge ego-trip). Ministry as well as Social Work has to be done with low expectations, otherwise it really can masquerade as an ego-trip. Do I know who can be saved or not? No. This is why we are given permission by our local Sheriff to enter his facility and begin the sorting-out process...which brings me to my next point.

Admiration for Law Enforcement

As a matter of fact I have developed a deep appreciation for those who serve in law enforcement, in particular those who serve this duty as their true calling in life, not as a power trip or game. The truly dedicated member of law enforcement has a nobility and dignity about them, knowing that they serve as a line of defense which literally prevents our communities from falling into a downward slide. Make no mistake, our way of life, our civilized society can veer off into the ditch at any moment with a brutal terrorist attack or food supply issue or viral crisis and truly, much of our social stability is truly dependent on dedicated law enforcement to keep this line of defense. Working with law enforcement personnel in Knox County (in particular the Knox County Sheriff's Department) over the past decade I have met the men and women who indeed have this nobility of calling and I have a deep respect for them and their sense of duty and dedication.

Law enforcement officers (to name a few who I worked with consistently at the Knox County Sheriff's Department) like former Sheriff Mike Morris, Chief Deputy Dan Mooney, Detective Mike Fisher, Sheriff

Doug Vantlin and former Jail Commander John Vendes have helped to teach me to stop thinking naively yet, yet have also given me enough space and independence to remain fully and completely a pastor. They didn't have to take this angle with me and I am forever grateful to them for this. They have always had a respect for our ministry and my role in their facility as one who is indeed a pastor. Yet they have never ceased to teach me to minister with my 'eyes' open. Under their leadership I have learned to toughen up and be careful. There are indeed inmates who are dangerous and need to be incarcerated, there will always be. In no way should any jail ministry go into a lock-down facility thinking that all of the inmates are merely victims of circumstance and that God loves them all and they just need a Bible study and/or a job and another chance at freedom. No. This naivete embarrasses me. I want no part of this type of Christian ministry. It is dangerous.

Judge Not

I have always had an admiration for local judges, even a reverence for them. They were at the pinnacle of leadership in every community I have ever lived and any time spent in a courtroom was very serious time indeed. My time doing the LAM Ministry meant quite a bit of time at the Knox County Courthouse attending various hearings for LAM participants. If I decided to appear in court for a participant and possibly testify on their behalf, it was a clear indication to the judge that I was willing to vouch for the genuineness and believability of that defendant. I learned to be in communication prior to a court hearing (whether it be a bond-reduction, trial or sentencing) with the judge and the prosecutor so that the court would take into consideration the LAM Program and in particular the LAM Houses as an option for sentencing. This is so key because the role of the

Judge and the Prosecutor are absolutely vital to being able to truly and I mean truly 'sort out' the inmates in the jail. A functioning drug rehab program or ministry must, must be in communication and good standing with the judges and the prosecutor so that they might help in the process of sorting out those in the jail who have been caught up in the system.

Knox County has three courts: Superior 1 and Superior 2 and Circuit Court. LAM primarily worked with Circuit and Superior 1. I recall learning so very much about the local judicial system from Superior 1 Judge Tim Crowley who was very patient with me as I began LAM. He was always supportive of LAM and always addressed me when I came to his court as "the reverend." After Judge Crowley retired and was elected to the County Council, Gara Lee was elected to take the bench and she was and still is amazingly supportive, having been an active attorney in many DCS (Department of Child Services) cases prior to being elected as Superior 1 Judge.

Judge Sherry Gilmore has been at the bench in Knox County Circuit Court since 1998. She is a wonderfully compassionate person and was always so aware of LAM and the importance of a proactive stance on inmate population reduction in our local jail. She always understood what I was doing and was always so supportive of me and Tania as we would come to her court, periodically throughout the year supporting this inmate or that, asking for permission from the court to continue what we started in the jail program. I cannot express more clearly how key it is that a program or ministry has trust and support from the local judges.

Dirk Carnahan and the Role of the Prosecutor

One of the most important people in local government is the County Prosecutor. Luckily, Knox County is gifted with a guy named Dirk Carnahan. He is a local attorney from a solid North Knox farm family who was elected as Prosecutor in 2016. I began to work closely with him as our transition houses became more and more a part of our ministry. I would take a short list of guys I was working with in the jail and ask him to let us house them at the LAM House as a part of probation or bonding or simply O.R. them to the LAM House (which stands for released on their "own recognizance"). The local county prosecutor is just as important as the Sheriff and the judges in our criminal justice system because they are the ones who set the tone, they begin the prosecution with a level of crime. They can choose to prosecute or not prosecute. They are an elected official so they are subject to the public, which means they can suffer in the public's eye if they are too soft on crime or are not prosecuting the right cases. This is a very important position. Dirk was always so kind to me as I would bring my little list of inmates to him and say, "Dirk, I want to work with this guy...let's see how he does." Dirk always honored me and gave the LAM guys a chance.

Indeed the local prosecutor is oftentimes overlooked as one of the key drivers in the increase in prison population. In his book entitled, *"Locked In: The True Causes of Mass Incarceration and How to Achieve Real Reform,"* Fordham University Professor John Pfaff gives a new perspective on other forces driving the increase in America's prison population. Pfaff claims that it is not drug offenses that are driving the increase, rather it is an increase in violent crimes and state and local prosecutors who are choosing to prosecute these violent crimes.[5] He goes against the common liberal storyline as proposed in the popular 2010 book by Michele Alexander entitled *"The New Jim Crow"* which says that this increase in prison population is driven by race. Pfaff would agree that we need to get low-level offenders out of the prison system, but the problem is much more systemic, much more violent. From the 1970's to the 1990's the increase in prison population was more a reaction to an increase in violent crimes, not just drugs. Professor Pfaff basically says that real reform means figuring out how we are going to punish violent crimes and not just drug crimes. Pfaff hits on a major theme which I find fascinating: the true area of reform is in the local area, not the Federal.

Pfaff points out that more than 90% of all criminal convictions are resolved through a plea agreement, therefore judges and juries have almost no say in how these crimes and cases are resolved, it is all done between the prosecutor and the local attorney.6 So this locally elected office is essentially one of the most important positions in the county when it comes to true reform. This is why much of our success at LAM was due to Prosecutor Carnahan and his willingness to allow our LAM participants to receive a chance at rehabilitation.

Professor Ernest Kurtz

I have outlined this book in such a way to give you a framework to understanding the process which has taken place to create this new community of recovering addicts. The outline itself is based on insight from my favorite book regarding the topic of recovery and Alcoholics Anonymous entitled "Not-God: A History of Alcoholics Anonymous" by a scholar named Ernest Kurtz. It is one of my favorite books in my entire 1,000 book library, period. To me, this was a game-changing book as it put the entire movement in historical and social perspective regarding 20th Century America. Professor Kurtz received his Ph.D. in the History of American Civilization from Harvard in 1978, 'Not-God' being his doctoral dissertation. In the opening pages of his seminal work, he states that Bill Wilson's idea for AA had four aspects to it:

1. Hopelessness
2. Deflation
3. Conversion
4. Full Human Interaction 7

I have taken these four points and have blatantly used them as the four walls of my house for the purposes of the expression of this present work. Everything I need to say will be contained within these four points, with the exception of this introduction. Professor Ernest Kurtz passed away in January of 2015. I want to thank him for the tremendous influence he and his meticulous research and passion have had on me, on LAM and this present work.

Part I: Hopelessness

"The core idea of Alcoholics Anonymous was primarily the concept of the *hopelessness* of the condition of alcoholism. That most people in mid-twentieth century America found this hopelessness most understandable couched in terms of "disease," "illness," or "malady" derived from the historical context and revealed more about the culture than about Alcoholics Anonymous."

Ernest Kurtz, "Not-God" page 34

A safe place for Brent

LAM began with hopelessness;

I do not remember the exact day but I recall a Saturday afternoon in March of 2005 in Westphalia, Indiana. I was preparing for the next day's worship at the local United Church of Christ, where I had been pastoring the small, rural congregation since January of 2002. A 13 year old youth named Brent who lived just a few houses down the road from the church and a member of our youth group came running up to the parsonage (sandwiched between the church and the 200 year-old German cemetery). Brent was startled and frightened and frantic. He asked if he could hide. I was stunned and alarmed. I asked him what was happening and he told me that someone was high on meth and chasing him around

Westphalia in his van. Sure enough, I looked outside and spotted a white van cruising the pot-holed streets of Westphalia. Brent hid behind the couch for quite a while...I remember looking down at him and we made eye contact. He seemed so hopeless and so did I. I had no idea how to help him...oh and btw, what was 'meth'? He asked me if he could stay for a few minutes longer. In a few minutes the coast was clear and he walked (or snuck) the tenth of a mile to his home. The next day he came to church and youth group as if nothing had happened. We never spoke of that moment again, as I from time to time see Brent around town and around the county as he resurfaces in different stages of his own debilitating and tragic cycle of addiction and (now) mental illness. But (whether he knows it or not) that moment changed the course of my life.

After Brent left the parsonage that day I realized that my ministry had changed: if my life as a pastor was going to be relevant and our church was going to be relevant to our community's needs then this issue needed (maybe not the incident itself) to be addressed. I remember after Brent left and I was left standing there in my living room, trying to return to my sermon preparation...but I couldn't...what a joke. Ministry seemed like a game to me then...what good was "the church" if people were suffering around me and I had no answer for them? I was saddened, deeply saddened. It also terrified me. It was real and sustained and it wasn't going away. What did he face when he got home? What would this person do to him when he saw him next? As a single Dad I would do anything to protect my son from harm, but what about Brent? Who was there to protect him (at least at that moment)? And how many more kids in Westphalia, in Knox County were hopeless like that? I needed to do something but all I could do was say, 'I'll pray for you.' Really? That's all I had?

A Safe Place for Brent

Westphalia, Indiana

Let me tell you a little about this small community where I was living at the time, the little town of Westphalia. I was pastoring Westphalia's United Church of Christ congregation for about three years at that time, having moved there from Chicago after my son Dylan had been born. My ex-wife Desiree and I had lived in Chicago for three years (1999-2001). The experience of Dylan's birth and the traumatic experience of '9-11' in Chicago changed our perspective and we headed home to family... yet I loved living in Chicago! I had just left one of the best jobs I had ever had working with the homeless who have a mental illness on the streets of Chicago at an organization called Thresholds. We left a city of 2.3 million to a town of 199 souls. Salem (with an attendance of about 70 on a good Sunday) was the only church in Westphalia. A bit of a culture shock, right?

The residents of Westphalia had established themselves as amazingly loyal, stoic, patriarchal, rigidly self-disciplined and frugal farmers of German lineage who did whatever it took to succeed at working the land day and night all year long. Although I was an outsider (from English and Scotch-Irish lineage) I decided to stay. But I really felt trapped, the divorce leaving me with few options since I needed to be near my toddler son and his mother.

Knox County is a mixed bag of influences, with the main town of Vincennes having distinct French and Native American characteristics such as place names and the layout of the town itself in relationship to the Wabash River instead of a rigid grid. The rural towns which dot the North and South of the county have a distinct stoic German influence with a tough work-ethic. In particular the North has areas like Westphalia which were founded by hardy German immigrants in the 1840's who had come directly from Germany. But, like any community it has its weaknesses and addictions have an uncanny way of exposing these weaknesses. There are pockets of immense, Appalachiaesque-poverty and social degradation

47

throughout our county, worsened by the cunning and baffling and hidden nature of chemical addictions. As you will see, meth swept in and completely exploited a not-so-secret weakness of the very species we call *homo sapiens*: addiction and our overwhelming desire to escape the boredom, fear and pain of this earthly existence.

As it turns out, wherever our species has roamed in its long and complicated quest to conquer space and subdue nature [1], addiction and its myriad of issues has tagged along. Indeed, every civilization, country and tiny community has had its issues with addiction. Most of these are just hush-hushed, the victims ostracized and marginalized.[2] To be sure, some countries and communities have had a long and extensive history with addiction, with drugs of choice which are a part of their national identity. For other civilizations and countries, their addictions are less engrained into the fabric of their society. Some communities deal with these issues relatively well with acceptance of boundaries in terms of use and misuse, while other communities go all-out Puritanical and label addictions as this dirty, moral problem of this fallen, physical existence that should be solved with a healthy dose of God, Bible Study, will-power and a good job.

Until Brent came running up to my door I had never given any of this any thought. I was thirty-five years old and I had never even thought of these issues before. At 35 years of age, I began to realize how sheltered my life had been and how easy my life had been. When Brent came running up to my home to hide, I was confronted with this little secret my community had been hiding all along with the rumors of child neglect and abuse which tag along. I would soon discover that my neighbors and the people who sat in the pews on Sunday morning, these people were now dealing with a drug which could not be well-hidden like pot use or alcoholism. Pot heads and alcoholics were good at hiding their addiction but meth addicts...not so much. Meth was brutal and it was available, easily available and so effective at alleviating this existential angst very, very quickly. Meth began to take people down hard and quick. As a pastor in this little German community I began to see these issues of addiction for what they really were; they were impacting the helpless children and youth whom I was serving as their shepherd. I had been at Salem UCC for 3 years and was growing bored with the mundane nature of small parish life. Much of church work can be simply maintaining a social club with preaching, calls, Bible studies and the occasional wedding and funeral. Yet I was never far away from the general feeling I had as their pastor: I wasn't one of them. I never (even when I left in 2007) felt that I was truly 'one of the family.' Their church was full of wonderful people (many of whom I still call friends). We loved each other as well as we could but full membership into their German family was impossible.

Was I an outsider? You bet...on the Sunday that I was voted in as their pastor, I was approached by an old farmer; a burly, bully leader in their church for years and years. He 'greeted' me on his way out of the after-church all congregational meeting he whispered, "I never have liked you and I never will." His meek wife made no eye contact with me as she followed him downstairs into the "Fellowship Hall" for a reception for me and my family. The church sometimes has nothing on the local jail. There are thugs in every walk of life.

No Shepherd for the Addicts

Ah, the church...the church in Westphalia (as a closed-system) was fine just as it was, it didn't need changing. It just needed to be reassured that they were on the 'right side' of heaven each week and they would be fine. They really weren't interested in doing any outreach into the community. But I saw something different. I saw pain and suffering. After Brent came up to my house a light was turned on in my darkened mind. I realized that there was no concerted effort by the local church or the faith-community at large to address these issues of ministry to those with addictions, yet the signs were everywhere that our community was in crisis.

Indeed the occasional evangelical church offered a 'Jesus-only' approach. The local mental health provider offered their equally myopic medical-model remedy (i.e. more medication and court-ordered classes for 9-18 weeks) to address the systemic issues of addictions in the specific community where we lived. There were also the ubiquitous 12 Step meetings which served as a life-line to so many addicts and alcoholics since 1934 which met at various locations throughout our county. But there was nothing concerted, nothing organized at a grassroots level. There was definitely nothing to address the issues which were arising from the arrival of this new drug called 'meth.' It was not enough to say, 'We will be praying for you,' or 'All you need is a job and a place to live.' The answers which ministry and Social Work were offering were not enough by themselves. Ministry and Social Work needed to merge their heart and their hands and combine the best of both. In that merging, there was the answer.

I remember once that I spoke at a nearby Chamber of Commerce in an adjacent county which had invited LAM to speak at their annual meeting. There were about 40 or so in attendance and after a nice dinner we convened in a little auditorium that served as the site for their community theatre. A couple of the LAM participants and veterans of our program spoke and told of their road to recovery and the importance of having a jail program. Then I got up to close-out our talk. I asked those in attendance if they had a jail program in their jail. After a few seconds of silence, an older woman with her white hair bunned-up neatly on her head blurted out that they had a local pastor doing a Bible study in their jail. I decided to be very frank and I opened my mouth and said, "A single Bible-study is not enough. You can't call that a program. As a matter of fact, I'm not sure a community can call itself a 'Christian' community if it does not have a drug-rehabilitation program in its local jail." You (literally) could have heard a pin drop in that auditorium.

I remember leaving that talk (very, very soon after we had finished) and driving out of town. I did not mean to be rude, but in my heart I believed what I had said and I believe they needed to hear that. I believed it and I still do: if a community or a country is going to label itself as 'Christian' then you need to be in your jail offering a drug-rehabilitation and housing program. It all starts in the jail. The jail should be the very first focus of every church in town and city in America, large or small, rural or urban or suburban. The county jail is the primary mission field of the church in America. I contend that it is one (if not the most) neglected, violent and hopeful places in every American community, urban and rural and suburban. In each county jail sits the root of our ills as a society. If we can attend to those in each jail who have fallen through the cracks then we can heal in ways we didn't even know we were sick. Our country needs a healing and it needs that healing badly.

The Invaluable Influence of Social Work (and what ministry was missing)

Much of the inspiration and experience for what I have done with LAM has been due to the influence of a largely secular movement within our country, namely that of Social Work. Indeed (specifically the United Methodist Church) the church has been where I was lovingly nurtured as a child and teenager, but it was the practical-approach and overwhelming compassion of Social Work which gave me my drive and my voice as I grew into adulthood. The church provided me with no such drive and voice. The field of Social Work gave me the actual experience with practical work which the ministry lacked (and still does to a large extent). My colleagues at Thresholds in Chicago get the credit for this influence, the likes of Amy Ferrara and Christina Campbell, John Murphy and Bob Fredrickson...these are the dedicated workers who labored in the trenches with the truly underserved and suffering homeless and mentally ill who survived in a violent and unforgiving city ravaged by racism and inequality and apathy.

51

The Social Workers I worked beside in the back-streets of Ravenswood and Lower-Wacker Drive and Wrigleyville and Andersonville, these people were as Christian as any Christian minister (or Christian for that matter) I had ever encountered, yet not a one of them preached or proselytized about his or her own viewpoint on God or god. Indeed we talked little about such labels. There was no need. Indeed there was no time for such talk because there were people to serve, people in need, people who were suffering.

It was here in Chicago that I realized there was something missing in the Christianity of my experience. What was missing? What was missing was the connection between a personal, spiritual experience and the organic 'work' which naturally proceeds from such spiritual action within the psyche.

> *"What good is it, my brothers and sisters, if you say you have faith but do not have works? Can faith save you? If a brother or sister is naked and lacks daily food, and one of you says to them, 'Go in peace; keep warm and eat your fill,' and yet you do not supply their bodily needs, what good of that? So faith by itself, if it has no works, is dead."*

James 2:14-17 (NRSV)

I have a deep respect for the profession of Social Work and their work-ethic. When you truly find a dedicated Social Worker you have found someone who is dedicated, deeply dedicated to what they do...they believe in what they do because something within them drives to get up each day and do what they do, regardless of how our society treats them or the people they serve. They just do it and do not have to be patted on the back and given a treat. They just do it.

I have worked twice as a Social Worker yet would never label myself as a Social Worker since I do not have a License (LCSW or LCW) nor do I have a Masters or even a Bachelor's Degree in Social Work. Yet in my five years of working full-time in Social Work I gained this respect, much as I have in the jail setting with those in their calling to the profession of Law Enforcement. Social Workers are very similar in this sense of calling. No one (for certain) is called to such a profession for the enormous perks or high salary or the pomp and prestige. One must be dedicated on a similar level as Law Enforcement, being driven by a desire to help those who are underserved and suffering from abuse, neglect, prejudice and poverty.

There are so many different areas to work in when it comes to a career in Social Work such as;

- Child Welfare
- Mental Health
- Public Welfare
- Health Care
- School Social Work
- Elderly [3]

Yet any type of Social Work field focuses its attention on those who are underserved and neglected. This is the fire and the focus which is so badly neglected within Christianity today. Christianity has much to learn from Social Work, needing to revive its non-existent inner prayer life and merging it with a dedicated, mission-mindedness which Social Work provides. Social Work, while providing this anthropocentric viewpoint, has at its teleological end the goal of healing society itself, working one person at a time. What a great way to see the world!

It's all about the ideas here. Let's look at some of the ideas within the field of Social Work which drives this movement toward action. One of the most basic ideas within Social Work is the anthropocentric view. In other words, this field is primarily concerned with assisting humanity adapt, adjust and thrive in their own living environments. People are the focus. The first approach which Social Work offers is to assist people and/or a population adapt and adjust to their environment. This is termed the 'Micro-practice." The second approach of true Social Work is assisting the environment itself so that a population can adjust and adapt and flourish, which is termed the 'Macro-practice.' Either way, people are the focal point, helping them adjust and flourish in their own environment. 4

In my own work in the Social Work field, I have been involved in the micro-practice of assisting those who are homeless who have a mental illness to adjust and flourish. As I have alluded to, I gravitated toward Social Work because of my personal disillusionment with the profession of ministry. I struggled immensely in my late 20's and early 30's in what my 'call' to ministry looked like, with a very combative and surprisingly complicated relationship with the United Methodist Church and their process of ordination. I have since processed through this struggle yet for a time (quite a time actually) I felt as if I was done with ministry, at least in the form it had and was taking in my own life. My time at Thresholds was invaluable in giving my call to 'Christian' ministry a voice when the church offered none for me. I remember starting my work in Chicago with Thresholds and the homeless who have a mental illness and literally saying, "I want to do Christian ministry without the preaching." I just wanted to do without having to tell anyone, "Hey...I am doing ministry here, look at me." Could I be 'Christ' in their midst without having to say so?

I was determined to try. My personal call to ministry, however, was not diminished in the least. I continued to want to serve and be useful as I had always had a genuine experience of the love of God within my life. Enter the profession of Social Work into my life, casting me a lifeline when I needed it most. Social Work gave my call to ministry a 'voice' when I felt I had none left and for that I am forever grateful. In many ways my work in LAM is a testament to the functioning of Social Work in my professional life, hence my desire to voice my opinion that this amalgamation of the two very, very similar professions should be working more closely together, fulfilling both their missions with equal zeal and excitement.

Any typical Social Work textbook in any college bookstore will tell you a similar story: social workers are asked to work out in society itself, attempting to alter the social structures within society so that society itself can heal for the sake of humanity and creation. The first social work movements in the U.S. were called the Charity Organization Societies (COS) and were formed in the 1870's as a way to focus attention on the expansion of our industrial-based economy and the enormous impact of that expansion on human beings. Poverty became a focal point because people were getting left behind, forgotten and manipulated by the drive for profit by the Capitalism run-amok. Although this early movement utilized the micro-practice instead and focused on poverty being a 'character-defect' by the individual in poverty, attempting to root-out poverty one person at a time instead of the macro-practice of attacking the industrial system itself. 5

The Settlement Movement of the 1880's with the Neighborhood Guild in New York City and the Hull House in Chicago directed by Jane Adams was another trailblazing movement within the burgeoning field of Social Work. This approach was more based on the macro-practice with the idea that in order to help poor people rise up out of their condition of poverty the Social Worker herself or himself had to live within the community itself and provide services within that community. In other words, a person's well-being was directly linked to external surroundings such as improvement in the living conditions. 6

Either way, Social Work began on a mission: to help people where they lived. This approach is called the "person-in-environment perspective" where the underserved are given attention because they have been partially or completely forgotten and abandoned by a society driven by the economic needs of the rich and powerful. 7

In terms of the theories within Social Work there are some fascinating ideas:

- General Systems Theory; developed in the early 1970's describing the functioning of a living system where each separate part functions independently of the whole system but is also dependent on the whole system. This system looks at people in terms of all the systems and how this interaction impacts the lives of people.
- Ecological Systems; this approach looks beyond the focus on the client and examines the larger environmental context, where the individual and their environment interact.
- Strengths Perspective; the focus is not primarily on what the individual lacks, rather the focus is on what strengths they possess. This focus isn't on what is wrong, but what is right.
- Diversity Perspective; the emphasis here is on the rich diversity of the social workers and the clients which brings empowerment and change to a community. This implies an understanding of the community itself with its beliefs and biases, knowing and understanding the dynamics of oppression and discrimination. [8]

It is fascinating to me to realize that LAM truly utilizes bits and pieces of each approach in our ministry as a whole. Indeed, the pioneers within the field of Social Work such as Mary Richmond and Jane Adams saw a sense of hopelessness in the people they served. It was the search to alleviate this hopelessness which drew them toward this work. This search to address the hopelessness of the individual human life is what drives LAM, as well.

October 30, 2009

One of the main ideas which drove LAM when I was the Director was this: working with one person at a time. When we take this tack, we are able to utilize the best idea from the profession of Social Work as well as the best idea from Christian ministry, namely the idea that when you heal a person you heal more than just that one person. When a person is healed the entire community around them gets healthier and healthier. *By healing the sickest of the sick in your community, something happens, something happens to the health of that community...the 'tide is turned,' so to speak.* What happens is this: you have the entire community beginning, just beginning to heal on a social and spiritual (psychological) level far and above anything they have seen prior to the sickness. The social and spiritual ramifications are endless.

This idea of healing one person at a time began with one person in the LAM ministry: William Heuby. Let me tell you his story; on October 30, 2009 William entered the Life After Meth (LAM) Drug-Rehabilitation program at the Knox County Jail in Vincennes, Indiana. He had a nobility about his appearance: six foot four, long arms, short, trimmed crew-cut and piercingly intense eyes. He was clean shaven and neat in his appearance yet his 45 year old face showed the deep grooves and battle scars from thirty plus years of continuous drug and alcohol abuse. I couldn't tell if he was angry or just naturally intense. Either way there seemed to be an urgency about him, a desperation and a hunger, but mostly just anger. I knew he was a 'ringer' (a term I picked up from my training days with the Center for Therapeutic Justice directed by Morgan Moss and Penny Patton to describe an inmate who is sick and tired of being sick and tired and ready to join a recovery program).

Following the protocol of initial jail-staff approval and our LAM interview process (with me and three current team leaders), he was admitted into our little community tucked away in our own 16 bed cell block [the newly constructed Knox County Jail had eight (7 male and 1 female) cell blocks called pods and held approximately 225 inmates]. For the first six weeks he continued to be, angry, intense but he became more bitter, arrogant and angry with each passing day. Something wasn't right with him. For the first 60 days he was a nominal member of our community, doing the bare-minimum work in order to stay in the pod.

He was the consummate underachiever like everyone else in the program (or the jail for that matter). By mid-December he had grown more bitter and angry, to the point that he was disrupting the entire program for everyone else. Each passing day saw him more obstinate and skeptical, something had to be done. Finally, I met with my three team leaders and we made a decision to speak with William. We decided that a private meeting with William must happen in order to give him an ultimatum: either change your negative attitude or you will be removed from the program. 9

On December 16, the team leaders and I met with William in the classroom at the Knox County Jail (down the hall from where the LAM Program was housed). We spoke to him frankly and he spoke to us frankly. It seemed as though his negative attitude was not going to change, so reluctantly I agreed with the team leaders that he needed to be removed. I would tell the guards to move him as soon as possible.

As we walked back to C Pod we stood waiting for the guards to electronically open the door to C pod. As we stood waiting, William pleaded with me to give him one more chance. He began to bargain with me: he asked if I would give him 48 hours to improve his attitude...he said that if he continued to be negative then I could remove him, no resistance on his part. As he bargained with me the team leaders (all three of them) looked at me and knew that I was going to fold and give him the 48 hours to try and improve his chances of staying in this 'honor program.' Even though I looked weak and a typical pushover, I said yes to his request.

A Safe Place for Brent

December 18, 2009

On the morning of December 18, 2009 I made my way to the LAM Program in C Pod at the Knox County Jail to attend the morning group at 8:30 a.m. As I hit the button for the guard at the central command station to buzz me in, I couldn't wait to see what had happened to William. Had he continued his negative ways or had he truly improved his attitude so much that everyone agreed that he should remain in the program? As I opened the heavy, metal door and the latch was still buzzing open I was met at the door by William. He had a blue copy of the Alcoholics Anonymous 'Big Book' in his big hands and he stuck it in my face and said, "Have you read this stuff? It's all in there. All my answers are in here!" he smiled, poking his index finger on the side of his head.

January 26, 2010

On January 26, 2010 I appointed William as one of the team leaders for the LAM Program. His attitude had continued to progress, becoming more and more positive. He began to teach several of our classes, in particular leading those regarding the 12 Steps. He also began a natural progression toward leading other participants in their recovery. He began a key role as a sponsor for several participants in the program, helping them take the next step in their recovery. In doing so he began to realize something: he was being helped just as much as they were being helped.

In the months to come, William and I had several opportunities to speak one-on-one. These individual counseling sessions gave me a glimpse into his life, so filled with heartache, abuse, resentments and anger. This was my first, up-close look at someone in recovery. What I saw astonished me:

- I saw how amazingly difficult and complicated it truly is to recover from years of alcohol and drug abuse.
- I saw how muddied a life can become when the abuse and the neglect begins in early childhood.
- I saw firsthand how the scars left behind by abandonment and addiction can be permanent.
- I saw that a truly emptied and broken life can only be healed by allowing a 'higher power' *into* that emptied and broken psyche.
- I saw how the presence of neglected children can motivate a parent/addict into doing brave and courageous things in order to try and salvage and save those same neglected children.

William and I began a friendship based on trust and desperation and hope. He began trusting me as he saw that although I was indeed green and inexperienced I was there, sitting in front of him unafraid and free, offering my support to another human being in need. This unearned trust would have to be earned the hard way: time and sacrifice.

Over the next few months and years we would continue the ups and downs of a new relationship. We began a friendship in the milieu of a county jail surrounded by the drama only a small-town county jail can bring. Mostly we sat and talked about regret and new life, God and the deeply mysterious nature of life and meaning and what true freedom looks like in someone's life. We would always, always talk about his children and their well-being and his desire to get out of jail and return to them. More than anything he wanted to be a father to his son and daughter (who were in the third and fourth grade at the time of his last incarceration). This desire burned within him.

I was determined to help him return to his children.

A Safe Place for Brent

February 18, 2010

On February 18, 2010 LAM had its first annual banquet. It would be the first year of our annual fundraising event. We had decided that the main speaker at each banquet would be a LAM participant or participants. In the first two years of the banquet we got permission from Sheriff Mike Morris to bring a male, LAM inmate (along with an officer) from the jail to be one of our main speakers. I chose to bring William to be one of the two speakers at our first banquet (Tanner Buttrum was the second LAM speaker that night and he had settled in Evansville after his release from the Knox County Jail).

We convened at the First Baptist Church in Vincennes with about 220 in attendance. Jimmy Morrison (from our LAM Board of Directors) catered the fried chicken meal and all went well for our first banquet. When William got up to speak, I was so excited and curious to hear what he had to say. He had his 'awakening' just two short months prior and he had been such a positive influence on the program. We had spoken of what he was going to say that night, but neither of us really knew what he was going to say when he rose to the podium. He opened his mouth and spoke.

He began with a summary of his life and how he had found his way to the LAM Program at the Knox County Jail. He gave us ample examples of the abuse and neglect that he had experienced as a child which led him into a three decade-long adult life filled with equal amounts of abuse and neglect. As he began to finish his remarks he spoke of the guilt about his five children, but especially his two youngest who were still in elementary school in Vincennes. They were both in attendance that night, sitting a few feet from the podium where William stood and spoke. He said that his three decades of outlawing and drugging had accumulated some serious felony charges and that he would most likely have to serve some amount of time in the Indiana Department of Corrections (he ended up being sentenced to four years in the Indiana Department of Corrections).

As he said this, he looked down at his two youngest children and looked at them and said, "Even though I have to go to prison, I will return for you. I will be back for you." With those words he ended his talk. All 220 of us in attendance sat, stunned, every person silenced by the natural and unfolding story we were honored to be witnessing. It was one of the highlights of my entire experience with LAM as I realized that this was just the beginning of William's transformation. I was determined to help William return safely to his children. No matter what, I wanted to help him return home.

The Long Wait

William would indeed be confronted with the harsh reality of a long prison term, one which would see him serve four years in the Indiana Department of Corrections. Initially he was sent to Branchville Correctional Facility down in Tell City, Indiana. He began to write me letters, all of which I have saved and read through once in a while to get a glimpse of the severity and isolation which awaits anyone who is incarcerated. In one of his first letters dated February 8, 2011, William writes,

> *How are things? I hope this reaches you and finds you and your family well. As for myself? It's bad here, Pete. God is here, but He's sure hard to find in an individual, man to man basis. I keep praying for guidance and I know I have a purpose here, but it's really tough.*

He asks how the program is going...how this participant is doing and that one...he asks for a reference letter so he can apply for a therapeutic program in prison so he can get a time-cut...then he ends his letter with this,

> *It hurts here Pete. It hurts my spirit. Pray for me, please. Much respect, William.*

William H. and his children...

William taught me the true meaning of working one person at a time. He did this by working on himself. After spending a few months at Branchville Correctional Facility, William was sent to Plainfield Prison where he would spend the remainder of his time in prison. He continued to write me and I wrote back (although not nearly as often as he would like, which he made abundantly clear to me). He became involved in hospice care for dying inmates as well as drug rehabilitation programs (which offered him a nice time-cut). His letters reveal an existential urgency, not only to reach his children but also with God. There was this sense that he needed to make up for lost time that he needed to find his purpose as a human being. Above all, there was this sense of intensity which I had never seen before in a human being. On January 23, 2012 he writes,

> *So how is LAM? Still operating? I do know that had LAM not been there I never would've awakened. I would still be trapped in these useless, self-destructive cycles that have repeated over and over in my life. I also know that where LAM is located, and when is vitally important. We both know that true growth comes through pain and when you have an addict, still suffering withdrawal, so afraid and hurting and expose them to the opportunities in LAM it can have an amazing effect. Anyway, in my life, when I let go, I found that God had me the whole time.*

He ends his letter with this,

My children need me desperately Pete. I need to go home to them.

A Safe Place for William

On January 2, 2014 William H. was released from the custody of the Indiana Department of Corrections. He was released with his parole destination being the Life After Meth Transition Home in Vincennes, Indiana. I was waiting for him at the LAM House.

We had done it, we had prepared a place for him with:

- a warm house
- running water
- a clean bed in his own private room
- television and access to the internet
- an appointment at St. Vincent de Paul's thrift shop (wonderfully operated by the five Catholic churches in Knox County) to get three new changes of clothes
- an appointment with a job coach from KCARC's Dove Employment Services.

Yet the first thing that we did that day was visit his children, who had been staying with his mother until he could obtain custody of them through the Knox County Superior Court system.

I took a picture of them all together, standing huddled around one another in his mother's house on the North End neighborhood of Vincennes. The look upon William's face was one of sheer exhaustion. I knew of the pain, but didn't understand it, yet his children understood this pain. They understood because they had suffered with him for the last five years. For five years his children did not know what would really happen. They didn't know if he really meant what he was saying. He had said he was quitting before and they had been disappointed every single time. Why should this time be any different?

A Safe Place for his children

In June 2015 William H. moved out of the LAM House and into his own rented home about ten blocks from the LAM House. Shortly after he was released in January of 2014 he obtained a custodial job at Vincennes University. He quickly excelled at that job and began to move up the 'ladder,' eventually landing a well-paying job at VU in the Maintenance Department as an electrician (William had an impressive work history and a great many skills that he had somehow managed to achieve during his active addiction days). He also began working with the court system and the Bureau of Motor Vehicles toward re-obtaining his driver's license. He was an active member of the 12 Step community as well as the LAM Support Group, becoming it's president in 2015.

We spent many hours talking about his overall plan. You see, his plan wasn't just to get a job and get his license back and be a 12 Step sponsor. All of these achievements were toward a greater goal, the goal of having his own home so that he could have a safe place for his children. One of the most amazing attorneys I have ever met (and member of our LAM Board of Directors) is named Jonathan Feavel. He represented William as he slowly built his case to get custody back of his children. He wanted to show (not tell) Judge Sherry Gilmore that he was indeed ready and steady as a father. He wanted the court to see that he had done it, he had done what he said he was going to do: return to his children and take up his role as father. He wanted to live a life of peace, filled with the natural highs from the normal joys, sorrows and frustrations which come from being a parent. He wanted to live, plain and simple, he wanted to live.

In August 2015 Judge Gilmore signed the custody papers which gave William H. complete and legal custody of his two youngest children. On October 22, 2015 William and I went to have lunch at a Mexican Restaurant in Vincennes. I picked him up at VU during his lunch break. On the drive there we both spoke of the ups and downs of living in a house with a pre-teen and a teenager. We laughed at the similarities in our houses with the drama of undone chores and blank stares at questions regarding homework and tooth brushing and dirty clothes in the hallway. We laughed. Two fathers laughed at ourselves, at our children, at our common, plain and simple lives that we were leading. We laughed. We will meet again soon, probably for lunch and we will talk about other mundane things which fathers have in common as we try and find the best way to love our children the best way we know how.

In a letter William wrote to me from prison on January 29, 2012 he wrote these initial words,

> *Pete, Hey, How are you? I hope you and your family are all well and in great health. I am well. I am homesick and I miss [my children] terribly. I have placed them on that secret shelf within my heart, but still...*

William is now home with his children. He does not have to be homesick anymore. He has fulfilled his promise to his children, to God and to himself. He is home.

This is why LAM does what it does.

Check out what he said in a LAM NA meeting at the jail on November 20, 2017;

The main thing is I don't hurt anyone anymore...I don't do drugs, I don't drink...I work and take care of my kids and I live my life. All I know is I don't hurt anyone anymore.

The Children Are Suffering

My professional and personal experience with William Heuby and his children has given me a stark reminder of the true victims of drug and alcohol abuse in this country: the children. While William was incarcerated for those four long years I stayed in touch with William's mother, who had custody of his two youngest children. I recall the great experience every Christmas as Tania and I were involved in the delivering of Christmas gifts to his children, donated by a local, loving anonymous citizen. For three straight Christmas seasons we delivered gifts to them, but the happiness on his children's faces was always tempered by the longing for the one true gift: the return of their father.

Because of my experience with William and the impact of his incarceration on his children, the issues which has driven and will always drive me in this ministry is the issue of drug abuse and how it impacts the lives of helpless and hopeless children. If your community is like Knox County in Southwestern Indiana you can testify to the fact that the drug crisis (especially since methamphetamine came on the scene in the late 1980's as it crept across our country from Southern California) has taken its existential, economic and environmental toll on our families, our churches our schools and our children. Take a look: in our county alone, the CHINS cases or 'children in need of services' went sky-high since 1999;

New CHINS filings (according to Dena Held, Director of Knox County Court Appointed Special Advocacy Program):

1999	2000	2001	2002	2003	2004	2005	2006	2007	2008	2009	2010
20	21	55	62	54	80	56	52	122	140	141	200

In a twelve year span our little county witnessed a 10x increase of children who were in such a personal crisis that the county government needed to step in and help them with the basic needs of existence: food, clothing and shelter. These children could not survive in the conditions that they were living in and the local government had to step in and help.

Here are statistics from Knox County Superior I Court (one of three courts in Knox County) under Judge Timothy Crowley (retired in 2014) regarding the ratio of total number of criminal cases in his court and those involving meth and cocaine during the same years of increase in the number of CHINS cases (1999 through 2010);

<u>Year</u>   <u>Total # of Criminal Cases Filed</u>
<u># of meth/cocaine</u>

- o 1999   10/0   60

- o 2000   50/0   139

- o 2001   126/0   218

- o 2002   145/0   185

- o 2003   182/6   231

- o 2004   152/4   209

- o 2005   103/8   215

- o 2006   50/5   84

- o 2007   35/3   82

- o 2008   63/22   117

- o 2009   87/0   137

- o 2010   109/1   161

There is an obvious correlation between the remarkable increase in the number of children living in chaos and in need of assistance and the equally remarkable and disturbing increase in the number of criminal cases and corresponding increase in meth cases. The increase in children in desperate need of assistance was in direct proportion to the increase in meth-driven criminal activity in the same time period in the same county.

Lynn Rump and Tina Hidde from the Southwest Indiana Regional Youth Village hosted a panel-discussion on the Opioid crisis in our community (February 9, 2017). At this well-attended event at our local Fortnightly Club in Vincennes they shared some fascinating statistics from the *Indiana Youth Survey 2016,* sponsored by the Indiana Prevention Resource Center. Let me share a few of these stats which are related to children and the impact drugs and incarceration have on them; 10

Students were asked:

- "During any time in your life, has either of your parents or guardians served time in jail or prison?"

	7th grade	8th grade	9th grade	10th grade	11th grade	12th grade
Knox County	29.7%	29.7%	32.1%	31.4%	29.1%	34.4%
Indiana	20.8%	24.4%	22.7%	22.4%	20.3%	19.0%

Students were asked several questions regarding their mental health:

- "During the past 12 months, did you ever feel so sad or hopeless almost every day for two weeks or more in a row that you stopped doing some usual activities?

	6th grade	7th grade	8th grade	9th grade	10th grade	11th grade	12th grade
Knox County	23.1%	33.1%	34.4%	37.0%	33.0%	37.5%	33.6%
Indiana	21.5%	23.1%	28.0%	30.5%	31.2%	30.7%	29.1%
U.S.	n/a	n/a	n/a	28.4%	29.8%	31.4%	30.0%

- "During the past 12 months, did you ever seriously consider attempting suicide?"

	6th grade	7th grade	8th grade	9th grade	10th grade	11th grade	12th grade
Knox County	12.0 %	17.0 %	24.3%	23.4%	23.1%	21.6%	17.9%
Indiana	8.5%	12.8 %	16.9%	18.0%	17.3%	16.9%	15.2%
U.S.	n/a	n/a	n/a	15.0%	15.4%	13.9%	13.8%

As you can see from these startling statistics from the survey and from courts statistics, a significant portion of our youth report having major stumbling blocks placed in front of them during the most delicate and dangerous years of their entire life: adolescence. I mean adolescence is difficult enough in a stable family life, let alone with a parent(s) absent and the depression, isolation and social stigmatization settling in around them.

LAM's own statistics from the LAM Program are significant as well with the average age of drug and/or alcohol onset being **13 years old** for both the men and the women participants. Additionally, the average number of children born to them, (which means that stat excludes any step-children) is **two children**.

When these pre-adolescent and adolescent children begin to look around for help, for relief, for shelter, for guidance...for anything, what do they find? I have a one-word answer for what they find: *stigmatization*. They are 'embraced' by a society that (for a myriad of reasons, some of which we will explore) deals with the complexity of addictions by creating a rigid set of rules, boundaries and penalties upon those who violate them. These rigid sets of rules **are** important to set for some within this at-risk population. As I said before, there are some anti-social, pathologically criminal members of our society who will never be attracted toward living a life of self-fulfillment and civilized behavior. Yet we are not talking about this segment of the drug-culture. The LAM ministry is interested in the segment (the vast majority of this drug-culture population) who are **not** inherently deviant. Rather, LAM (as should any community which would like to consider itself a 'Christian' community) is interested in reaching into the jail and helping those who are lost and trapped. We are interested in helping them escape this trap before they are institutionalized, before the trauma and stigmatization have physically altered their minds.

The Stigmatization of Alex

One of the motivating factors which energized the LAM ministry is the fight against the stigmatization of addicts within our community and our country. I recall when I began this ministry, the mere mention of drug addiction or the reference to someone who had succumbed to drug addiction oftentimes evoked a similar response to some in our community: forced pity followed closely by repulsion. In short, addicts were looked down upon as lazy, morally weak weights upon society who just couldn't get their lives together long enough to hold down a job like the rest of us. Alcoholics were another category with a little more leniency given to them since our community had such an ongoing and complicated relationship with alcohol, alcohol being the drug of choice of so many within our community. But drug addicts, that was another story.

When the meth crisis hit our community in the early 2000's the term 'drug addict' was reserved for the sub-culture of post-70's hippies and veterans of the war in Vietnam with their pot and the Vincennes University students from far-away places like Gary and South Bend and Indianapolis with their crack cocaine and occasional heroin. In short, drug addicts and their 'moral weakness' were not a front and center problem for Knox County. Was addiction a problem for our community? Sure, but it could be handled, hidden and moralized away on Sunday morning, the self-image of our clean and tidy community all put back together with aphorisms and quotes from kitchen-table calendars. The problems that did occur were hidden within families or behind the bars of the Knox County Jail, when it was located across the street from the Knox County Courthouse in downtown Vincennes until 2007. But the arrival of meth changed everything for Knox County, so much so that by the time I became involved in LAM in 2005, the Knox County Council (the branch of local government within the counties of Indiana which is similar to the legislative branch, dealing with county finances and budgeting) was planning for a major jail expansion on the outskirts of town with the jail population increasing from approximately 80 to 225. Meth was such an egregious and fast-acting drug (in terms of an addiction) that it could not be hidden. The impact of meth began to quickly dismantle an addict's life and the life of their children within a matter of weeks, resulting in the complete obliteration of family, job and social structure of an addict within a matter of 6 months. Alcoholism, on the other hand, could be hidden and 'controlled' for ten, twenty and thirty years, the undulations of that chemical addiction being much slower and much, much more socially acceptable than drugs. Meth pushed the social envelope on addiction.

On a social level a community has to often struggle with its own self-image. Our community is no different. We still struggle with this issue of how to *socially* treat drug addicts and alcoholics within our community. This issue of socialization and addictions within a community is something which interests me greatly. How is it done? What does it look like within our social structure? Is this structure healthy?

I believe one of the main ways to de-stigmatize a social ill is to *personalize* the stigmatized. In other words, put a face on the problem. One of the main reasons LAM has been and continues to be a ministry within our jail and our community is because so many people within our community have been touched by addictions, whether it resulted in incarceration or not. I would dare say there is not one person within the 38,000 plus population of Knox County who has not had some contact (whether family or friend or co-worker, etc.) with the disease of addiction in one shape or form. Everyone knows someone with this disease and they are baffled by its cunning patterns and its severity and swiftness. One of the issues which continues to drive the LAM ministry is the de-stigmatization of addictions on a social-level within our community.

Let me introduce you to a LAM participant who was greatly stigmatized by the label of 'drug addict' when he was in the 6th grade. His name is Alexander Ray. When I met Alex he was a 25 year old kid, sitting stoop-shouldered, blonde hair flowing over his face, ready for his interview to get into the LAM Program. At such a young age, it was hard to believe that he was already a veteran of the United States Army, but he was. Or maybe he was lying. That part didn't bother me, I just wanted to see how much pain he was in, how 'done' he was with this whole life of addiction and incarceration and isolation.

I recall distinctly sitting in C Pod around the circle of 18 other inmates and listening to him comment during our Anger Management course about how angry he really was, and he wasn't kidding. He was terribly angry, angry at the U.S. Government or his family or his so-called friends who had already abandoned him in jail. He was just so very angry, this manifesting itself mostly in his political views, which interestingly enough bordered on Socialism with a tinge of Lenin and the early, vibrant days of the Communist Revolution fighting against capitalism. I knew one thing about Alex: he was a thinker, highly intelligent with an unusual sensitivity toward issues of justice and equality. He had a compassionate heart, much bigger than most Christians I had met, frankly, but oh, how he was wasting his time and talent on all the tied-up emotional knots he had been working on since an early age. He was a twisted mess, unable to let his true talent and love flow out of him. But somehow he knew he had something to give to the world, something more than just a statistic. More than anything, I could see that Alex was a fighter. He wanted to find out why he was so twisted up. It was my job to settle in with him and walk beside him on his journey to begin untying these knots. [Isn't this what ministry and Social Work are all about?]

He stayed in the program, never violating any rules or being disruptive to the community. When he left the program and was released from the jail into our community he decided to come to the LAM House for a while. His stay at the LAM House did not last long, ending in his expulsion from the house for drug use. Relapses, by the way, should never, ever be taken personally, so after he was expelled we stayed in contact. As a matter of fact, he and I really began to develop a friendship after he was expelled. I needed back-up though so I tried to connect with my good friend Professor Jesse Coomer over at Vincennes University's English Department. Alex was an avid reader and writer, who would often share some of his ideas and writings with me while he was in the jail program. I saw an opening here and decided to call in Jesse to see if some outside encouragement from a pro would help, so Jesse and I decided to start a writer's club, meeting at the local 'I'mpressed Coffee House' which lasted only a few sessions.

I wouldn't give up. Even with the dissolution of the writer's group, Alex and I remained connected. I had no idea if he was clean. Soon he told me he had met a girl there at Vincennes. She lived in Fort Wayne and soon he moved away with her to her home town. But we continued to stay in texting contact. As I finished my first novel in 2016 I shared it with him and he read it and responded so kindly to it, even traveling back for a visit to family and taking time to have lunch with me and share his thoughts. To this day I have never had anyone encourage me about my writing more than Alex did that day at Procopio's Pizza. We remained in contact and still do, our friendship growing with each passing conversation. We reconnected on May 9, 2017 for breakfast at the Olde Thyme Diner on Main Street in Vincennes. His 18 month old son Finn squirmed and wriggled as we spoke about life, his new life as a sober father seeing the world with brand new eyes. Now he can begin to see his past, making sense of the chaos and where it all began. He spoke openly about some of the issues he was faced with as an adolescent, loosening and untying some of these most difficult knots;

It was 1999 and he was in the 6th grade at nearby South Knox Middle School (one of four school systems in Knox County). He was in his first year at the school and knew very few kids, joining band to try and fit in. He recalls getting an ounce of hash from a kid and not even knowing what it was or how to use it. After the authorities began asking questions he decided to do the right thing so he turned himself in to the Principal of the South Knox Middle School. But to his shock, this Principal decided to let his honesty amount for nothing, the Principal making an example of Alex and sending a clear message to the other students, faculty and community. Alex was expelled for the remainder of the year. He was forced to be absent from school for one and a half semesters. He quit band, lost friends and was immediately labeled as a druggie kid who was immediately shunned. The label was impossible to shake.

By the 9th grade he had transferred back to the Vincennes School district where he attended Lincoln High School. Alex says, "When you start out as a child and you're cast out as a black sheep you choose either love or drugs and I chose drugs and all my relationships became toxic for a long time…and I still get angry, get angry at rich people even though I know they are going through the same things I am…I was outcast by Christians too…they aren't acting out of love and love is the only thing that leads you."

Our breakfast wasn't as long as we had hoped, with little Finn squirming around and needing to walk around. As we settled the bill we walked out of the Olde Thyme Diner and onto Main Street there in Vincennes, he stopped and looked at me and said, "Reestablishing someone's self-worth is the greatest thing you can do for someone...you know this program saved my life Pete." He paused and looked down at Finn and said, "I have everything I need right now." He grinned and said, "Wanna see a trick?" He picked up little Finn under his arms and hoisted him up and carefully began to place his small feet in the cupped palms of both his hands and he began to balance Finn. Finn looked at me and (literally) smirked, as if to say, "...yea man, watch this...we do this all the time, me and Dad..." Right there on Main Street, Alex balanced his toddler son in the palms of his hands, Finn knowing exactly what to do to keep this balance...for several seconds they balanced before Alex slowly lowered him to the ground and quickly scooped him up into the waiting car seat for the long ride back to Fort Wayne. After he buckled him in his car-seat, we hugged and promised to remain in contact, to continue to share our stories and ideas and lives. I watched him pull away and drive toward Second Street and then north. I stood there amid the quiet May morning in downtown Vincennes and looked around. Before I headed to the Knox County Jail for the Anger Management group, I treated myself to a walk around downtown, not a care in the world.

Knox County's Methamphetamine Crisis

Socially speaking, the scene was set for a systematic stigmatization of drug addicts within our community. So when meth began to surface in the mid-1990's in Knox County, our community had an old paradigm set in place to deal with a new problem. The problem was, this new drug and all the other drugs it brought with it was much more powerful and effective, rendering the old paradigm of shunning and criminalization terribly outdated and damaging. People like Alex began to fall through the cracks at an early age as our community and many like it began to apply old policies to a new problem. This impacted the social structure of our entire community. The dominos began to fall, one by one.

As I've discussed in the Introduction, LAM seeks to help the specific addicts who have become trapped in their disease of addiction, literally trapped in jail as well as trapped in the cycle of the disease itself. The reasons some of them have become trapped was out of a desire, a desperate desire to escape the trauma of abuse, the boredom of existence, the pain of abandonment or the need to feel a part of a family or a group of any kind. This next section will talk about the physical and psychological trap which awaits anyone who seeks solace in a bottle or a needle or a foil.

I cannot tell you how many times I have had people around the county who are *not* suffering the disease of addiction ask me (some honestly and some pretentiously): "Why would anyone do that to their body?" In particular they ask this question after I answer the questions about what ingredient goes in the 'recipe' of meth and chemical make-up of meth and how it is manufactured and used by an addict. As a non-addict I try and answer this question with a focus on the pain and suffering that the addict is escaping from, but we human beings are odd creatures, right? We have a wide gap between knowledge and understanding. Prejudice and fear are quite powerful, in particular when they are focused on the black sheep of the family.

One of the ways I have come to understand this issue of 'why?' is to be in frequent conversation with the addicts themselves, which understandably is not available to many people. I have that luxury. One ex-LAM participant from the early days of LAM in 2008 was especially helpful in opening my eyes to a very practical and philosophical reason why chemical addiction is such a consistent characteristic of human existence. His name is Ralph Chambers. I spoke with him at the Knox County Jail in early 2017 while he was serving out his time in the jail as a trustee doing kitchen duty. He is one of the old timers. He was born in 1962 and began using alcohol and weed in 1970 or 1971. He started using meth in 1975 at age 13. 1975 was the year the Vietnam War came to a close, the Watergate scandal was at its apex and the nation dealt with an unbelievable influx of drugs and drug addicts. Ralph is a survivor, a very practical man who took a few moments with me on the last day in January of 2017 and spoke honestly to me about his four decades of drug addiction and incarceration.

By the time he was 8 years old he was drinking and smoking weed, but when 'Crystal' hit town and he tried it, it was a feeling above and beyond what beer and pot gave him. Meth made Ralph feel "invincible," giving him an energy which helped to temporarily erase the stressors of his 13 year old mind. He said, "Everyone has depression and we all want to feel good and meth makes you feel good...plus it is illegal and makes you feel like a rebel doing illegal stuff."

He said he doesn't recall meth being manufactured locally until about the year 2000, this is when it all changed.   This is when a drug like meth could be manufactured for use as well as for profit. Meth changed it all.

Why Meth Changed It All?

As LAM began its ministry in 2005 it was clear very quickly that meth was not our only problem. We even talked briefly about changing our name because we knew it wasn't just about meth. The hysteria and mystery surrounding this new drug was at its pinnacle yet we had other drugs already in our area such as alcohol, pot, cocaine and heroin which had been around for years. Methamphetamine was just the 'flavor of the month.' It was clear that we would be dealing with addiction issues from a myriad of drugs, not just meth. Yet meth was a 'game-changer' for us. It opened our collective eyes to the dangers and destructive nature of addiction as a disease, not just a moral shortcoming. Now (at the time of publication) we are dealing with K-2, spice and 'bath salts,' not to mention a drug like 'krokodile' which hasn't hit us yet. But in our little corner of Southern Indiana, this onslaught of new, synthetic lab drugs all started with the introduction of a synthetic stimulant called methamphetamine.

Methamphetamine and its slightly older, chemical cousin amphetamine had very humble and quiet beginnings. Ephedrine (the active ingredient in amphetamine) was first developed by a German chemist named Lazar Edeleano in 1887. Methamphetamine was synthesized by a Japanese pharmacologist named Nagayoshi Nagai in 1893 and then again by Akira Ogata in 1919. [11] For all practical purposes, both drugs were developed without a specific need. In other words, amphetamine and methamphetamine were drugs in search of a disease. In the early 20th Century they were prescribed legally for a myriad of ailments. According to Weisheit and White in their work (2008) on methamphetamine, these synthetic stimulants were used to legally treat more than thirty ailments, including:

- Narcolepsy
- Asthma
- Epilepsy
- Fatigue
- Depression
- Schizophrenia
- Alcoholism
- Morphine and codeine addiction
- Nicotine addiction
- Barbiturate intoxication
- Enuresis (bed wetting)
- Radiation sickness
- Sea sickness
- Dysmenorrhea (painful menstruation)
- Colic
- Obesity

- Persistent hiccups
- Stimulation of sexual libido
- Hyperactive children 12

Early on the medical community gave its blessing to the drug, specifically citing it as non-addictive. 13 In the 1930's and 40's these stimulants were primarily used to treat obesity and depression, but also as an over-the-counter drug to treat fatigue. 14 This acceptance by the medical community gave the general public an understandable sense of well-being regarding both drugs. The drugs really eased their way into the general population in the 1930's, laying a trap as the addictive qualities were greatly underestimated.

Nowhere is this more evident than in Nazi Germany. Drugs and their relationship with war and combat performance is no exception. World War II was particularly filled with events and decisions which impact us today, drugs included. The global conflict which ensued and has burned its way into our 21st Century has impacted us in many, many ways. One of the influences of WW II (both the Axis and the Allies) is the support of and the development of and wide distribution of amphetamines and methamphetamines to its military personnel and to the general public. In a book called "Blitzed: Drugs in Nazi Germany" (2015) by a German author named Normal Ohler, his extensive research suggests that a form of methamphetamine called 'Pervitin' developed for the Nazi Government by the Berlin-based pharmaceutical company Temmler-Werke and was widely available to German citizens as early as 1937. Pervitin was chemically close to what we know today as Crystal-Meth. 15 Opiate-based drugs such as heroin and the natural stimulant cocaine were viewed by the Nazis as too common and low-class...too 'Jewish.' The Nazis quite literally were racist even in their selection of their drug of choice, and in many ways this choice led to their steep and rapid decline during WW II. In a classic example of his overt racism, Hitler needed a new, pure 'Aryan' drug, one which would be suitable for the Aryan people. It was used (without a prescription) by common housewives, day-laborers and taxi-drivers just as caffeine is used as a stimulant.

According to Professor Lukasz Kamienski, the effects of methamphetamine were more intense and longer-lasting than those of amphetamine, the impact of meth on the body "similar to adrenaline, a hormone and neurotransmitter produced in the body" ...with an increase in..."self-confidence and willingness to take risks; sharpens concentration; enhances alertness; and significantly reduces hunger, thirst, pain sensitivity, and the need for sleep. All of these properties, highly desirable for the military profession, made Pervitin a perfectly appealing stimulant for German troops, particularly in the opening stages of the Second World War." [16]

The side effects after the drug intake is halted were so egregious that the Nazi Government itself banned Pervitin's use to the German public by 1941 but continued its use within its military. The famous Nazi General Irwin Rommel used Pervitin on a daily basis but more importantly, it allowed the Nazis Army to advance very quickly in their Blitzkrieg (Lightning War) in the Sudetenland, Poland and France. [17] In terms of effect on their soldiers and the speed of their advance through Western Europe, the German military gained more territory in 4 days compared to what it took them 4 years to do during their trench warfare of World War One. Pervitin was mixed in chocolate bars and widely distributed to their Luftwaffe and Panzer crews, in particular.

The Allies (U.S., Britain and Russia) as well as the Japanese took notice of the Nazi strategy and began to investigate the possibility of distributing these synthetic stimulants to their soldiers in order to compete on the same scale as the Germans. The American National Council for Scientific Research (NCSR) began to conduct research, leaning heavily on recent studies to enhance performance by athletes in the 1936 Berlin Olympic Games. According to Professor Kamienski, before the NCRS could make a recommendation to the U.S. Armed Forces, the U.S. Air Force ordered large amounts of Benzidrine or Amphetamine in late 1942.

The reality of the phenomenal military success of Nazi Germany in Western and Central Europe "loosened the breaks on ethics" and caused the Allies to apply the same or similar drugs to their unsuspecting and patriotic soldiers. [18] Consequently, between 250 and 500 million Benzidrine tablets were ordered by the U.S. government for distribution to its servicemen, increasing morale, mood, fortitude and aggression. [19]

The Surge and Conrad Harrell

The encouraged and promoted use of amphetamine and methamphetamine during WWII caused the first 'Surge' of the drugs in the late 1940's and early 1950's, in particular in the U.S. and Japan. Use of meth in post-war Japan and the U.S. were two contrasts in causation. America's surge of meth use began with returning soldiers to an affluent, post-war, baby-boom culture where this new 'pep pill' became something of a fad. It began to spread to truck drivers, students as well as the new Bohemian sub-culture groups on either coast (especially the West Coast scene in San Francisco) where drug experimentation was new and growing in popularity.

One of the keys to understanding meth problem in the United States lies squarely in relationship to its systematic and government-sponsored use on soldiers during World War II and their subsequent re-entry into American Society. Let's talk a bit about this idea of re-entry, but rather than look upon this in a macro-point of view, let's look at it in a micro-practice point of view. In other words, I want to know what type of impact these macro-decisions (for better or worse) had on the 'little guy' on the streets. The enormous amounts of drugs which were consumed during WW II had a long-term impact on our society in the aftermath of and the subsequent after-shock conflicts in Korea and Vietnam. This dysfunctional and historical connection between drugs and warfare holds an essential key to understanding why our little county in Southwestern Indiana was hit so hard, not to mention our entire nation.

Let me introduce you to one of the 'little guys,' who was impacted by such decisions of national and international security. I have had the privilege to get to know an inmate by the name of Conrad Harrell. He is a 52 year old, sweet-talking gentle-giant of a man (he is 6'2" and 200 plus pounds) who is one of the most talented artists I have ever met (in particular: tattoo-art). Conrad grew up in a middle class family in San Diego, California. His father was an alcoholic who merely paid the bills for his family. He was always gone and when he was around he was physically abusive to Conrad and his brother. His mother was a closet-addict who abused pain medication as a way to survive her abusive marriage. She rationalized her addiction by saying that her drugs were medicine being applied to a pain, but the damage was being done, to her and her sons. His mother's abuse was psychological and emotional in nature and caused deep scars upon her sons.

Conrad was expelled from school when he was 15 and joined the Navy by 17. By the time he was kicked out of the Navy he was in full-blown addiction, selling and abusing drugs, meth in particular. He joined the Hell's Angels Biker Gang which supplied him with his crystal meth and began to sell weed and meth for them. He eventually joined the Mongol Biker Gang and continued to have an endless supply of pure crystal meth. In 1997 he left the Mongols and began to sell weed for another gang, which led him East across I-70 and into Indiana, where he settled in Terre Haute. Today he calls Vincennes home, settling down with his family here to be a part of a larger LAM family. During his last time in the Knox County Jail (he was sent here by Vigo County due to overcrowding in their Terre Haute Jail) he became involved in the LAM Program and began working his Steps in a deep and meaningful way. I sat down with him in January of 2017 and talked to him about his upbringing in Stockton. He gave me an idea of the after-effects of this re-entry of soldiers into American society, saying that biker gangs played an enormous role in the spread of methamphetamine in our country. In particular, the infamous 'Hell's Angels' biker gang, according to Conrad was founded by WW II veterans returning to civilian life. Other biker gangs began to pop-up in the United States with the 'Outlaws' forming in Chicago and the 'Mongols' in San Diego. By the 1970's these biker gangs were staking out territory and dealing crystal meth as they headed Eastward across an unsuspecting American public with a completely unprepared system and paradigm of dealing with such a drug.

Conrad remembers growing up with his brother, just surviving a childhood with an alcoholic father who was a member of a biker gang and a mother who was a single-mom who was addicted to 'bennies.' 'Bennies' is the name of the upper his Mother was addicted to, short for 'Benzedrine.' Sound familiar? When he was 15 he remembers stealing money out of his Mom's purse and grabbing some bennies (sometimes called 'Yellow Jackets' or 'Cross-Tops'). By 15 he was expelled from school and began to sell weed and bennies. Both sides of Conrad's family are hard-drinking Catholics from Ireland, his first beer was a Coors Original given to him at age 9 by his grandma. By age 12 he was drinking on a daily basis.

Conrad is 52 years old and he is just now seeing his life and the screwed-up relationships he has inherited from his mother and father for what they truly are: completely and absolutely dysfunctional. As he has done Step Work and combined it with prayer and meditation, I have witnessed him blossom and grow into an amazing human being, one who is talented and gifted in not only his art but also his way with people. He has tremendous communication skills which literally could have led him down any path he so chose, but now, he is just trying to figure himself out. In a NA group at the jail once he said, "It's like I never came out of survival mode, like I'm a f*#!ing animal. I haven't respected myself for 52 years...What is love? We have a distorted image of love...I don't know what love is but I'll figure it out. I'll figure it out." During another session later that week we were talking about his upbringing and how he saw the world and how he related to 'the good people' of the world; "I have spent my entire life deceiving people. The only time I get angry is when I get caught deceiving you, that's when I get mad...I've done drugs with my mom and I remember one time on the phone my mom denied ever doing drugs ever! I love my mom but [forget] her I am 52 years old and I am sick of me, sick of not knowing who I am. Rock bottom just keeps changing for me."

Needless for me to say (as I am one who is in the trenches of this post-war impact) the decisions which men make have dire and dark consequences for many, many innocent people. I dare say, given different cultural circumstances, a man of the talent of Conrad Harrell could have achieved many things had not our culture been hijacked and injected by these nefarious influences from the 'castle on high.' But here we are, picking up the pieces, one person at a time, trying to heal our citizens, our communities, our nation one person at a time with the hope that by taking time and personal attention with the people who have fallen in between the cracks of our broken society that we can begin the healing process.

Has a man like Conrad Harrell done things in his life which warranted time behind bars? The answer is a resounding: yes! Yet I cannot tell you how many times I have sat in class and watched (in particular the older participants who are worn-out and tired) a LAM participant say: "Where has all of this recovery stuff been all of my life! I needed this stuff thirty years ago." But for many like Conrad, "Rock bottom just keeps changing for me." We need to be in the jails to sort-out those who needed this long ago but who never got it. We need to be in the jails to sort-out those who weren't ready to listen when they were young but are now sick and tired of being sick and tired. We need to be in the jails offering hope to the hopeless because there are people like Conrad Harrell who need to begin to contribute to society instead of draining society of its vital energy. Our society should be about lifting people up out of the muck and mire of a tangled and torn childhood. We need to help 'jumpstart' our society by helping those who indeed have been trapped in their past so that they can be lifted out of this and they can begin to contribute to the well-being of our society.

Facts about Meth

The use of meth in post war Japan was something quite different. Prior to World War II, Japan had a long tradition of warfare and nobility, fighting wars and psychologically maintaining the structure within their society through the idea of fighting a 'just war.' But World War II changed all of that for Japan, impacting their society for decades to come. Post-war Japan was extremely vulnerable to their meth surge due to two reasons: firstly, they were a defeated and demoralized country after four years of devastating war and their ultimate defeat came from two atomic bombs which further humiliated their country; secondly, there was a major over-supply of methamphetamine in Japan (which had been used heavily within the Japanese military), which eventually filtered down into the organized crime syndicates in post-war Japan, literally fueling their rise to power. [20]

In our study of the impact of meth upon Knox County, Indiana, we are interested in briefly tapping into the comparison between the economic and morally devastated state of post-war Japan and the similarly weakened social and economic condition of the American Midwest during the 1980's and 90's. Economics have a part to play in these surges of drugs within societies. During this period there was an economic upheaval in the rural economies of many American Midwestern communities. These communities saw much of their agrarian-based economies suffer as many family farms had to be sold or liquidated under stiff competition with larger, corporate farms and rising costs of equipment as well as fluctuating prices of grain and beans. Knox County was no different. As we have seen, Meth had been around for several decades, slowly infiltrating the general population through use within the military as well as various medical treatments. Meth was just waiting for an opportunity to fill the social and economic vulnerabilities of other parts of our culture.

Meth was (relatively) easy to make with one of its main ingredients easily found in farming communities. This key ingredient in the production of meth is called *anhydrous ammonia* and is still used today by farmers to fertilize their soil. This fertilizer is contained in large white tanks on farms and co-ops all over Knox County. These tanks could be tapped (which is called "riding the white buffalo") with a great risk of burning from the frozen state of the gas itself. All of the other ingredients for meth can be found at your local Wal-Mart or drug store such as CVS or Walgreens.

So not only can you make meth yourself and supply your own drug needs as well as make a good profit from selling the rest (if you want to share), meth-use itself gives you a feeling of unending energy and confidence, bordering on invincibility. You feel like you can do anything, achieve anything, be anything you want. As we have already stated, meth gives you a feeling of invincibility. Its major impact on the user is a huge release of dopamine in the pleasure center of the brain (up to a 1,400% increase in dopamine). With cocaine, this dopamine release is similar, but there is a major difference between the impact of cocaine and meth. Whereas cocaine opens up the release of dopamine into the synapse, with cocaine this dopamine is quickly taken back into the receptors of the brain (this is called 'reuptake'). Meth on the other hand (as well as amphetamines) *blocks* the reuptake of the dopamine, essentially keeping the dopamine in release mode into the brain, even blocking the enzymes within the brain which help breakdown the dopamine after it is released. Therefore, what you have is a longer, much longer high with meth as opposed to cocaine. A cocaine high can last for 15-20 minutes, whereas a meth high can last 2-3 days or more on one dose. The after-effects of such a potent release of this neurotransmitter is fatigue, irritability and depression. [21] Meth can worsen already existing conditions, such as poor oral hygiene and poor mental health. Meth mouth (the egregious rotting of the teeth and gums) usually occurs in meth users who already have poor oral hygiene before they started using. Likewise, if someone has a history of depression, bi-polar or schizophrenia (or any issues with mental health) the use of meth can not only worsen these symptoms but can leave the user with a permanent spiral of degrading mental health, the voices they now hear being endless and vicious whispers.

Methamphetamine posed(s) a major problem to communities for several reasons. Let's talk a little about the differences in this issue...Why was meth so popular in Knox County? Several factors contributed to methamphetamine's popularity in Knox County:

- **Potency**: a dose of meth (oral, intravenous or inhalation (smoking a 'foil') will increase dopamine by 1,100-1,400% and will last for 2-3 days (oftentimes the user will be up for more than a week or two with very little sleep within that period of time. With repeated use the user can be awake for as many as three weeks at a time, with an hour of sleep here or there during that period...one LAM participant told me he was up for 41 straight days once). This type of increase in the natural neurotransmitter within the human brain will provide the user with a sense of well-being (nearing invincibility and complete self-confidence).

- **Weight-loss:** a reduction in appetite is a common characteristic in meth use. Meth can be legally prescribed by some doctors as a weight-reduction drug called 'Desoxyn.' In the local, Knox County lingo if someone loses a significant amount of weight due to meth use they are said to be on the 'Jenny Crack' diet. I have known many middle-class members of our local community who became meth addicts because they initially wanted to lose a little weight. They ended up losing their careers and their families and some of them lost their life.

- **Availability**: a batch of methamphetamine can be 'cooked' from a recipe whose ingredients can be found easily on the internet and at local stores with an investment of about $200. This batch can be sold on the streets for approximately $800-900 and can also supply the cooker with a source for his or her own drug needs. Meth quickly became the new moonshine, ready to control a product for use and for income. When a user becomes his or her own supplier of the drug and the 'income' for their family then an entirely new world opens up for the addict. This means that any means possible will be met in order to supply the drug and the money, the drug and the money, and on and on. Coupled with the drug's physical damage to the frontal lobe of the brain (responsible for determining 'right and wrong behavior') inevitably leads to lying, cheating, stealing, burglary, weapons and illegal firearms possessions and all forms of violence known to humanity. This naturally leads to violations of the law on many, many levels and the subsequent arrests, sentencing and jail and prison terms which follow.

- **Chasing the Dragon**: oftentimes the first rush from a first-time use of meth can be such a life-changing event (never ever to be duplicated). In some women the first use of meth is orgasm-inducing. To someone who has been sexually, physically and/or psychologically abused, this is an enormous issue. This relationship between meth-use and sex (involving pornography or not) is often ignored. Yet I believe it is a key characteristic of meth use which is amazingly destructive and widespread. The ramifications to sexual abuse and the exploitation of past abuses are endless. This oftentimes orgasmic physical reaction from the first use and its subsequent psychological effects are always and hereafter sought after with each use of the drug. But that first high is never repeated, and the addict forever 'chases the dragon.'

A Safe Place for Brent

Professor Lukasz Kamienski

As I began LAM in 2005 I came face to face with the reality of the physical and psychological impact of meth as well as the more subtle social stigmatization which drug addicts and alcoholics face in everyday life. It was an 'easy-out' for those in our community to rely on the old paradigm of 'lock 'em up' and disregard me and my work with LAM since I am not from here, i.e. I was not born and raised in Knox County. In addition, I am not an addict or an alcoholic. In addition to that, I am a preacher. I really had three strikes against me from the start. Many (at first) saw me with these surface definitions and concluded that I was a self-righteous (if not well-meaning), greedy preacher who was not in recovery from addictions, searching for a way to make a buck off the misfortunes of the poor and the less fortunate. I had an angle, so some said. But I was undeterred. As I have discovered in doing my own 6th Step of the 12 Steps, my personality exudes stubbornness and arrogance when certain people doubt me or make fun of me. I become very head-strong and committed when I perceive that I have been judged this way and my intentions have been ignored. These character defects can be quite unsettling but directed at the right angle, they can (I keep telling myself) be productive.

Regardless, I saw people in need of help and I saw the ministry begin to unfold in front of my eyes. I had my motivation. The further I chased the rabbit down the rabbit hole, the more I realized that there was something more at work here, more than just an isolated drug epidemic in Southern Indiana. There was an historical back story and I wanted to know it. There was local history and there was history with a wider lens. Why do we have such a problem with drugs?

I began to ask the questions about Knox County and the history of drug use in our community. However, there was nothing unusual or spectacular about the history of drugs in Knox County...just the usual with problems with alcohol and pot...cocaine here and there and the dirty little secret of pain killers and the 'prescribed' medicine from legitimate doctors and General Practitioners. But the meth epidemic was something different. The meth crisis in Knox County seemed historically attached to a larger picture within our country's history and indeed our world's history. I want to take a bit and discuss the idea of this larger, macro-picture of the drug problem and how that larger picture can have an enormous impact on real people.

One of the greatest resources I have ever come across regarding the history of drugs in our country as well as in our global history came from the recent book by Lukasz Kamienski entitled "Shooting Up: a short History of Drugs and War." Professor Kamienski is Assistant Professor at the Faculty of International and Political Studies, Jagiellonian University in Krakow, Poland. This book (published in 2016) has changed the way I think about the social history of drug use in our country as well as revolutionizing the way I think about the sinister and complicated relationship between drugs and warfare throughout human history (not just American history). I am using Professor Kamienski's work extensively as a springboard to express the ideas surrounding the larger social context of drug use in Knox County, Indiana.

Professor Kamienski has done an absolutely marvelous job at the articulation of an extremely complicated subject: the relationship between drugs and warfare. His thesis is clear, as he states in the opening, "Perhaps the practice of getting high by fighting men is as old as war itself." [22] The idea that our military (any country's military) is an actual *continuation* of that country's culture is an idea which permeates his book. Although I do not agree with every conclusion and evaluation which Professor Kamienski makes within his seminal work, I do however find his work an invaluable 'springboard' which allows us to dive into the idea that there is a deep and abiding connection between our cultural composition and health and the history of warfare and the impact on the men and women in the trenches who return to civilian life, changed for better or worse. I want to offer some insights Professor Kamienski offers regarding the stigmatization of drug use within society and highly recommend his work to anyone who wants a closer look at this connection.

The meaning of the word itself can lead to understanding

I think so much *understanding* can be learned from personal and collective *history*. This can be said of not only our personal lives, but the histories of our community, country and collective species. The same can be said of our language and words and the manner in which we communicate to one another. This is why I am always fascinated by etymology, or the study of words and their origins. Let's look at the history of two words which interest us greatly: 'drug' and 'addict.' I am interested in these words and their histories in the context of the social stigmatization and criminalization of drugs in our culture. The root word generally thought of as the basis of 'drug' would be the Greek word *'pharmakon,'* which is translated as meaning "medicament" or medicine. But Professor Kamienski points out that in ancient Greece (pre 6th Century BC), there was a person associated with this noun, namely 'pharmakos' which is translated as a human scapegoat. This person was usually a 'slave, criminal or someone disabled or ugly...used in state rituals-in public rites of cleansing and in ceremonies aimed at ensuring the well-being and good fortune of a community. The *pharmakos* was manhandled, bitten, driven out, and sometimes stoned to death. So, as the Hungarian-American psychiatrist Thomas Szasz argued, the root of modern "pharmacology" is not "drug" or "medicine" but "scapegoat."' As the practice of human sacrifice was abandoned (at least in that overt form) by the 6th Century BC in Greece, the meaning of the word *"pharmakos"* was transformed into *pharmakeus* and *pharmakon* which was translated as a medicine, poison or panacea. [23]

Now let's look at the etymology of the word for the word 'addiction.' The root word does not go back as far as ancient Greece, but it is a Latin word from ancient Rome. Here I will quote Kamienski's full paragraph,

Drugs have strong habit-forming properties, and their abuse can cause intrinsically harmful physical, psychical, and social effects; therefore, in most countries today, they are illegal and strictly controlled substances with very limited medical applications. The word "addiction" derives from *addictus* - a citizen of ancient Rome who, being unable to repay his debts, was deprived of freedom by the courts and delivered into slavery under his creditor. Intoxicants do indeed have a similar effect; they enslave with their addictive properties. [24]

According to Kamienski, addiction and the 'scapegoats' who are 'indebted' to a drug are criminalized by a society. Societies from all walks of history have the desire and need to control human behavior, and this is no different. [25] One of the reasons societies utilize drugs on their soldiers is extremely practical: to help them get through the horrors of warfare in order to be victorious. Plain and simple: they want to win. Drugs assist in the three main phases of a soldier's experience: the pre-battle fear, the performance anxiety during battle and the ever-present and debilitating PTSD after battle. Drugs are a practical way of fighting the fear of battle, the attempt to transcend his or her natural human limitations. According to Kamienski, the Ancient Greeks actually considered drunkenness as virtuous, connecting you to the gods and liberating you toward the consciousness of your own divinity. It is not the natural 'evilness' of the drug itself, rather it is that particular society labeling this drug or all drugs as evil and demonic and the subsequent criminalization of their use. This criminalization leads to stigmatization and incarceration and politicization of the disease itself. It is not until the drugs and the alcohol use by the battlefield-deployed soldiers get 'out of hand' in the aftermath of the battlefield use and begins to spill over into civil, acceptable norms and mores of society does a society begin to rethink its productive effects on the soldiers performing on the battlefield. As a political move or in survival-mode, a society attempts to control the behavior of these returning soldiers/addicts by placing the criminalization label on a drug or groups of drugs or all drugs. There it begins: the stigmatization and the incarceration phases, the pendulum ever swinging back and forth between wars and conflicts and returning soldiers who have survived combat, only to succumb to the ravages of addiction without the presence of life-threatening combat.

It is important to point out that there is no automatic, sinister motive behind a country's use of drugs upon combat soldiers (that does not include an opposing army's soldiers, however), at least on the surface. The conventional wisdom (which implies a great deal of trust in the motivation of a society and their government's armed forces, warranted or not) would say that a society utilizes drugs on their soldiers because they want to win their armed conflicts. Although a society, by its very nature does have a proclivity to want to control the behavior of it citizens, a military's use of drugs during wartime is very utilitarian and practical; i.e. it wants to win the conflict and to do so they need soldiers to perform, cope and maintain readiness on and off the battlefield and drugs help them perform before, during and after a battle. According to Kamienski, during the crucial years of World War II, the United States Government was awaiting upon the evaluation by the National Council for Scientific Research to determine if Benzedrine or amphetamine was safe to use on soldiers (drawing upon research done primarily to enhance the performance of professional athletes, interestingly enough). But the U.S. military could not wait any longer and by late 1942 the U.S. Air Force ordered massive amounts of Benzedrine. In the name of defending our country against a legitimately sinister enemy in Nazi Germany, the U.S. military subjected its soldiers to an untested stimulant. The only country during WW II that did not utilize amphetamines or methamphetamines on its soldiers was the Soviet Union, whose drug of choice was alcohol, in particular Vodka.

A country has a drug of choice?

The use of drugs by a country is very similar to individual preferences to certain drugs. Each country, like each addict or alcoholic has a preferred drug or drink, each country having a drug of choice, as it were, each country and each war having a different drug of choice. Take for instance, the use of opium during the American Civil War by the North and the South. Opium (either via Laudanum or Morphine or Opium itself) was the national drug of choice in the early 19th Century America. By 1830, Opium was the #1 prescribed drug in America, as it was the panacea for all physical and psychological ailments and moods. By the time the Civil War came along in 1861, Opium was used extensively on the battlefield, with particular use in post-battle treatment. The Civil War witnessed 2 casualties from disease for every 1 casualty from battle, so this preferred drug was given extensively, similar to anti-biotics in our present society. It was even the main treatment for *diarrhea*, which according to Kamienski, 99.5% of all Union soldiers suffered from, so you can well imagine the extent of the addiction issue which was unleashed upon America in the aftermath of the war. Kamienski cites Horace Day's 1868 estimation of the number of morphine addicts in the U.S. between 80,000 and 100,000. By the beginning of World War I in 1914, there were between 200,000 and 300,000 habitual opium users in the U.S. [26]

The U.S. military's drug of choice during the Korean War was amphetamine and methamphetamine. In fact, amphetamine or Benzedrine use in post WW II American society was rampant and widespread, looked upon by the medical community on par with a vitamin, as a harmless stimulant, particularly effective in curbing appetite and offering a non-addictive, invigorating pick-me-up like caffeine. It was available without prescription until 1951, but even then it was prescribed widely. Amphetamine tablet production topped 3.5 billion in 1958 and by 1970 it had reached 10 billion. [27]

The Vietnam War is described by Kamienski as the first true pharmacological war with copious amounts of drugs readily available from the 'Golden Triangle' of Southeast Asia (page 187). The U.S. military prescribed massive amounts of Dexedrine (a derivative of amphetamine with 2x the strength of WWII-era Benzedrine) given to units with special operations covering several days. 28 Thorazine (an anti-psychotic drug) was also being administered to combat soldiers in the hopes of reducing battlefield trauma. However, Thorazine on the battlefield merely delayed the trauma, increasing the PTSD and subsequent drug-use in post-war veterans (approximately 15% of all Vietnam vets had PTSD). Drugs were readily available and self-prescribed during the decade-long Vietnam War as a coping mechanism for many of the soldiers, trying desperately to maintain their sanity amid the chaos and the bloodshed of a war which in the end had very little strategic value.

For the Vietnam vet, returning to an at best indifferent and conflicted society was heartbreaking. The lack of patriotism regarding the Vietnam War and America's attitude toward the men and women who fought it was a horrible experience for the veterans to experience. This stigmatization, when coupled with drug use is a social crisis waiting to happen within American society. Look at the estimated numbers Kamienski cites:

% of U.S. soldiers on drugs;   1968: 50%

1970: 60%

1973: 70%

Estimates of drug use by U.S. soldiers: marijuana: 51%

Heroin: 28%

Psychedelics (LSD): 31%

29

Take into consideration that during the last few months of the wind-down of the Vietnam War in 1975, over 1,000 U.S. service men were returning home to the U.S. homeland every single day. The massive, instant influx of hard-core drug addicts (many of whom had PTSD and other psychological issues in addition to the addiction issues) upon an unsuspecting country is truly frightening. It is this type of issue which helps explain part, at least part of the reason why the 1990's and early 2000's saw a sudden meth crisis in our country...it really should come as no surprise that we have an issue.

President Richard Nixon

The present-day 'war on drugs' in the United States had its humble beginnings on June 17, 1971. [this date is a matter of historical interpretation] As a three and half year old child living in a middle class, Methodist parsonage in Connersville, Indiana I was completely unaware of the issues. Little did I know that I would be so impacted by this War and this subsequent 'war on drugs' that I would spend my formative professional years ministering to and trying to give solace to the silent victims. On that day in 1971, President Richard Nixon gave a special message to Congress which in an instant turned a potential risk into a real threat to American society. In response to the already evident influx of drug-addicted soldiers returning from Vietnam (the war wouldn't be over for another 4 years), President Nixon announced that "public enemy number one in the United States is drug abuse," [30]

In reality, what this looked like was mandatory urine screens for returning servicemen. Yet by exaggerating the threat, the consummate thuggish politician that he was, President Nixon's real damage was to the veterans, those who were addicts and those who weren't. The stigmatization of the drug addict became a national attitude. Kamienski quotes Nixon,

Thus Nixon warned that 'a habit which costs five dollars a day to maintain in Vietnam can cost one hundred dollars a day to maintain in the United States, and those who continue to use heroin slip into the twilight world of crime, bad drugs, and all too often a premature death.' This was not only a gross exaggeration but also a harmful one as the president frightened the society not with a threat (a real danger) but with a risk (a probable danger). He presented the risk as if it was a threat. Thus, in the public mind, the fear of an addicted veteran returning home and endangering an orderly civilian world was created. A new 'other' was born. [31]

The Vietnam veteran used drugs to cope with the horrors of a war not of his own choosing. Upon his return to the home he had been defending against the evils of a Communist world, he was stigmatized and categorized as someone who did not fit-in to American society. He was 'othered.' Returning veterans who had addiction issues were not welcomed home, let alone given any kind of treatment or opportunity to receive treatment. Their disease was criminalized by myopic and selfish politicians and the only treatment they would receive was prison, institutionalization or death. Their disease and its characteristics was labeled as un-American in that they were socially-dysfunctional and chronically unemployed (two very un-American traits), hence their very identity was robbed from them upon their return to America. They were labeled as lazy and immoral, just not disciplined enough to quit doing drugs and just get a job like the rest of civil society. Ironically, there was a survey of returning soldiers done in September of 1971 which reported that over 60% of all returning soldiers ceased all drug use upon return to the United States and did not resume use. President Nixon did not update his report to Congress. The bullet hit its target. [32]

A Safe Place for Brent

Part II: Deflation

"The second aspect of the core A.A. idea was that *deflation* arose from this perception of hopelessness. In the developing argot of Alcoholics Anonymous, a language that moved always from the possibly mysterious to the sheerly vivid, the term *deflation* was replaced by *hitting bottom*."

Ernest Kurtz, "Not-God" page 34

"As I sit and write these words on a beautiful May evening in 2017, our world aches and groans underneath its own weight. Our collective technology has outgrown our collective maturity as we can no longer sustain our outlandish growth and ecological collapse. Our oceans and forests and prairies are bending and buckling under this growth and we seem to be deaf to the moans and cries, save shallow and dated aphorisms mixed with cynicism, boredom and apathy and greed. We have wars and rumors of wars and they are deafening. We are quickly breaking-off into old, tribal groups, all in the name of our grandfather's God. For the open-hearted, open-minded human being, these pressures mount with each passing day. I close my eyes and pray for my children. What will they say of me?

I will awake to the same world tomorrow, the same egregious news headlines, the same tension and I will pretend that it has always been this way. I will take a deep breath and prepare my morning coffee and ascend the stairs to my third-floor study where I can escape from all the turmoil and strife. There, in the gaze of icons and my library I try and fill my mind with thoughts of higher things. I will gather my thoughts and try and repel the waves of fear and trepidation and, regathering my thoughts, again and again I will use the Jesus Prayer to fill my mind with thoughts of higher things, praying for an open mind as I prepare to continue my work at the jail and in our community. Then I will walk downstairs to my bedroom closet and pick out my favorite Christmas tie (to date I have 54 of the ugliest Christmas ties on the planet) to wear to work. I will walk out onto Perry Street and go to my all electric Nissan Leaf and drive silently to the Knox County Jail and start all over again, trying to be of some assistance to those I have been given care of, the people in the ministry my God has gifted me.

I will rise again and try and make a difference today. I will lend my hand to a world that has lost its image of God underneath its layers of pain and suffering and hatred. I will go to the main source of my community's pain and suffering and hatred and fear: the jail. It is in the jail that I see God transform this pain and suffering into hope and faith and love. The jail is the place where, as a minister, I find the true Spirit of my God in the lives of the broken down inmates who have seen enough of the pain and suffering."

That is a journal entry from May of 2017. As I finish up this memoir it is May of 2019. At the time I thought that I might continue with the LAM ministry for several more years but as it turns out, I myself became deflated as Karl Jung would say. On October 6, 2017 I had three LAM House residents relapse at the LAM Houses with an hour of one another. I recall being at my friend Trevor's home for a birthday party and getting the call at about 9:30...I wouldn't get home until well past 2 am, having to call a Federal Parole officer as well as local probation officers and call an emergency LAM House meeting with both the men's and women's home. After 10 years of experiencing the existential yo-yo effect of relapses I had finally worn-out. I was deflated. Within two weeks of that October night I was told by Rev. Steve DeFields-Gambrell that he was leaving his position at First Christian Church and the rest as they say, is history. Yet this journal entry captures something I wanted to convey: the importance of the jail as a sanctuary, as a place where you can 'capture' a human being who is in the condition of true existential deflation, as Dr. Jung defined the term. My deflation was just burn-out. I wasn't really 'deflated.' I have been deflated in my life twice before and trust me, you know it when you are there. The jail is a perfect place to catch fellow Americans who are ready to change, ready to join the civilized world.

While I was the LAM Director, the jail and the inmates and the hope of true transformation were my only answers to the problems that arrived at my doorstep each morning, laid at my feet like the nightly kill by my innocent, well-fed cat. The Knox County Jail was my refuge, my sanctuary, my odd home I was blessed with for over a decade. My accidental career gave me refuge from this uncertain world. In the Knox County Jail I found the kindest and most gentle men and women I have ever known. In the midst of a world which seems to know nothing of truth these days, I ran to it, this place of incarceration, this place of brutality and punishment, this place of redemption and irrationality in a world gone absolutely mad as it tries to find balance in the midst of a horrific, blind fall. In this place of punishment I found solace, I have found redemption, I have found the Spirit of my God alive and well in a group of throw-away men and women who have been discarded by a society innocently trying to find a balance in a world which is constantly spinning. In a word, I have found hope among the hopeless.

I found hope in the form of people, hope in their lives, in their eyes as I said to them: 'your life is not over.' I found them where I always found them, waiting for me to hit the button on E-pod or D-pod or B-pod (depending on where our program was housed at the time)and wait for the guard to buzz me through. Then, with my lanky arm I opened the heavy door to E-pod and watched them, making eye-contact with some, others look toward their feet as they all walk-out into the brightly-lit hallway and the newly waxed floors as we head to the classroom. (I imagine now, on a typical Monday) I would sit down with them and I would ask them, "Well, how was the weekend?"

It was there, at their point of deflation that we would meet, at their rock bottom I would meet them face to face... and it is here that I experienced my God most profoundly, that I found my God in the pock-marked and scarred and sunken faces and the bloodshot eyes of men who are worn out and tired, broken and emptied by a life pursuing nothing more than solace from this same world that I seek refuge from, this same fallen world still searching for truth and meaning and transcendence from this uncertainty.

I am no felon, nor am I a recovering drug addict or alcoholic. I have never even been in a fight (even in the jail), nor have I ever hit anyone. I am a pacifist at heart and practice, my small physical frame having given me a different perspective on the world. Yet I found that I am no different than the inmates, these criminals. I identified with them and wanted desperately to become a part of their life, having been invited into their suffering, having been invited into their pain. Some would scoff at that statement...different indeed, they say. Yet it is how I felt then and it is how I feel now. The only thing I really miss about LAM is the guys at the jail, being with them and listening to them.

Some of us *homo sapiens* are a looking for God, we seekers just search for this transcendence in different ways. It took an entire decade of work in the Knox County Jail for me to see this image clearly, that I am no different, that I too search for meaning and purpose and direction in my life. I found out that I had been searching for my God all of this time too. We were all brothers in this search and every morning I rededicated myself to the promise: I will help you find it too, I will help you find your direction and purpose and meaning...I will help you find your God. In this I discovered that I was healed, healed of my brokenness and my rebellion against this image of God within my psyche. Now in hindsight I realize I was granted direction and purpose and meaning in the form of broken and hollowed-out men and women sitting in the Knox County Jail. Their personalities were the fuel for my broken soul that needed to begin my own healing. Combined in humility we created an energy…fire. All along it had been my soul that needed mending, most of all. I was the broken one too. I was the one in need of mending.

I believe, truly and earnestly believe that the world can be healed when the most broken members of our society are loved. It is this simple belief that kept me going to the Knox County Jail for a decade. It is this same spirit of hope which is driving me to write this memoir, to tell the story of solace and peace in a world that is in desperate need of both.

And that is the brilliance of two broken people getting together with a common pain, finding solace and comfort for a few moments in their common suffering. That is the brilliance of the 12 Steps: the rekindling of the human spirit.

The Social Worker who taught me how to be a minister

There is one man who first showed me the brilliance and beauty of the local jail and his name was Delbert Boone. He was the one who taught me how to combine ministry and social work. He introduced me to the world of jail ministry where deflation is a pre-requisite condition of the heart, soul and mind; i.e. the psyche. He showed me this place that every county in the United States has located somewhere within its borders. It is the place to find the diamonds in the trash heap. He first introduced me to Bill W. and Dr. Bob and the 12 Steps of Recovery.

I remember when I first began working seriously on LAM as a profession in the summer of 2007 we were visited by Mr. Delbert Boone. He was introduced to me through Penny Patton and Morgan Moss. I give him credit with giving me the confidence to do LAM even though I am not a person in recovery from addiction. Toward the end of his first visit to the Knox County Jail in the summer of 2007, he said to another person but knowing I was in earshot: "Pete will be alright...he's diggin' at it." I will never forget those words of confidence. They have helped to inspire me all of these years.

He visited again in 2008 but I had lost contact with him. I was hoping to have him read and advise me on this present book about LAM but sadly enough Delbert passed away in the summer of 2016. I wish that we had made contact before his death so that I could tell him how much he meant to me, the influence that he had on me and this ministry. If I could have that chance to see him once more I would tell him that he was the greatest single influence on my ministry and he wasn't even a minister. He was the one who showed me that ministry and social work can be combined to make a powerful ministry. Indeed, the combination makes both stronger and more vibrant, allowing both to have a potency which neither one had in their potential. He was without a doubt the greatest Social Worker I have ever met, probably ever will meet. His work as an intelligent voice within a subject that he had existential knowledge of was a truly wondrous sight to behold. LAM has nearly a dozen dvds which have captured his legendary lecture and speaking style and we show them often in the program. The DVD of his lecture on Maslow's Hierarchy of Needs is a particular favorite of mine.

Delbert was a legend among the drug rehabilitation community. After his college education and Master's degree, he was a teacher and a parole officer before his drug use led him to serve four prison terms between 1977 and 1982. As a recovering addict and ex-felon he began a new program in Missouri called ESCAPE (Effective Substance Abuse Attitude Personal Encounter) which was eventually chosen as an official program for the Missouri State Prison system. ESCAPE won the United Way Program of the Year and in 1984 First Lady Nancy Reagan visited him for advice on her 'Just Say No' anti-drug campaign. He was the first to bring me this message loud and clear: **the county jail is the place to start**. During one of his visits he spoke at Community United Methodist Church (pastored at the time by Rev. Andy Kinsey who was a vital leader in the early days of LAM) for an evening community worship service. During that meeting at Community United Methodist Church he said, "People don't get well because they want to. People get well because they have to, so don't ask…tell the addict how to recover. These guys are not criminals. They have an illness. It is not a moral decision. It is a medical [issue]."

The talk that night changed the way I thought about addiction and treatment and altered the course of LAM and our ministry. It gave me the big picture, especially when Mr. Boone highlighted the American Medical Association's 1956 declaration that alcohol and chemical dependency is a DISEASE. The idea that changes everything is this: addiction is indeed a **disease** and *NOT* a **moral** issue. This changes how we do ministry, let alone treatment. It changed how LAM did ministry. I took copious notes that night…

Mr. Boone stated seven components to effective drug treatment, which we have followed throughout our ministry;

1) Raise awareness
2) Education k-12 (by 5th or 6th grade it is too late)
3) Coordinate policy efforts, i.e. national policies
4) Identify drug/alcohol addiction signs
5) Build strong intervention components
6) Build strong referral components
7) Site statistics and research in order to substantiate funding/grants

He went on to say that there are four disciplines which work on treatment:

1) Detoxification
2) Rehabilitation
3) Outpatient

4) Individual counseling...

{All of these must be done in conjunction with AA and NA. If an alcoholic or addict does any combination of these for at least two years, Mr. Boone stated that there was an 80% chance of holding onto their sobriety}

Addictions, he said, are incurable, chronic and progressive with the vast majority (nearly 95% dying from this cunning, baffling and powerful disease before they receive treatment).

As he finished up his talk he stated, "Addictions don't make friends, they take hostages."

Social Architecture

During his visit to Vincennes in 2008, Mr. Boone spoke eloquently about the need to look at the addict in a different light, a sociological light. He said that Bill Wilson (as the co-founder of AA) was one of the greatest *social architects* of our age. This idea intrigued me: social architecture. It still does. It is this idea which has kept me going for so many years, working with drug addicts and alcoholics as if our civilization depended on such work. It is the idea of looking at the drug addict in their potential, not their present condition or their past chaos. Because their past and present oftentimes look very grim and dark, no light at all coming from their smoldering ashes of relationships and physical breakdown. Yet the life of recovery looks at the present. Mr. Boone said "Yesterday don't count and tomorrow hadn't happened yet. I'm working on today."

Mr. Boone described addicts as creative, dedicated, resourceful, resilient and responsible. It was this type of thinking which made me realize that this wasn't just a ministry to make me feel good about myself in the midst of all my personal blessings. It was a ministry which was contributing to our decaying social fabric. It was a positive, loving voice in the midst of the chaotic cries for help in our modern world. It was an offering to those who cared about living a civilized existence. It was a step toward civilizing our feral existence in the 21st Century.

A Nation Incarcerated

As I began the LAM Ministry I realized very quickly that I was walking into new territory. The only thing I had going for me was that I was willing to try and help those who needed it most. I was naïve and annoyingly positive about the ministry in its early days. (I maintained my positivity but I learned to no longer be naïve) I am sure those in our community had to exercise a great deal of patience when they would hear me speak about what we were attempting to do with LAM. Who could blame them? I mean here I was saying that we were going to try and do something about a problem that has perplexed not only our community, but our state and our nation for over twenty years, namely that of the relationship between mass-incarceration and drug addiction. I wasn't even originally from Knox County *and* I wasn't even a person in recovery from drugs or alcohol addiction and yet there I was saying I had an answer to this particularly perplexing problem. I was an outsider in every aspect of my LAM Ministry, yet it didn't stop me. I felt drawn to the jail.

I was quickly humbled at how complicated this issue was to everyone involved, with no clear answers, regardless of where you were born, the color of your skin or your last name. This issue was so prominent in our community because it was touching so many lives. I believed in my heart that the faith-community needed to rise to the occasion and begin some movement toward a solution. This issue of addiction and incarceration is so large in our country that no one organization or politician or program has THE ultimate and final answer. I believe that each community has to work on a local level and apply several approaches to the problem, finding their own rhythm regarding their socio-economic and cultural background. If I have discovered anything for certain it is this: *the answers are all local*. This idea that the answers can be found on a national level to the problem of mass-incarceration and addictions, with all the toxicity of our collective dysfunction as a Nation is simply ridiculous. This is why a national pivot toward the Opioid Crisis is a hollow battle cry to me. This answer is not what some want to hear, but I firmly believe that each community needs to approach this problem with an eye on their own issues, addressing them locally. It is what we did in Knox County.

We Americans have a peculiar need to find **one** 'grand' answer to any given problem. This issue of mass-incarceration is no different. We want to find one answer that is the key to unlocking the door that is holding us in, one grand answer that releases all of our tension and suffering and brings relief and new life and hope. The issue of over-incarceration is no different. We want to find the answer and then move on to the next problem. We're Americans for crying out loud, that's what we do: solve problems! Yet here we are with the problem of mass-incarceration with no real answer in sight. Since the mid 1990's the U.S. has incarcerated more of our own citizens than any other country on Earth. On any given day in the U.S. 2.2 million Americans are incarcerated (that is 1/99 U.S. citizens). Paul Waldman reports that the Bureau of Justice Statistics cites some startling statistics when he writes,

> In 1992, there were 1.3 million inmates in America's prison and jails; by two decades later, a million more had been added...the majority of those-around 60 percent-are in state prisons, where most people who commit crimes end up. Only around 10 percent are in federal prison, despite the attention those prisons receive; the rest are held in local jails. And those don't include the millions more on probation and parole. At the end of 2011, there were 2.2

million Americans incarcerated, 854,000 on parole, and almost 4 million on probation, meaning just under 7 million Americans-or 1/34 adults-were being supervised by the criminal-justice system. 1

Former President Obama has pointed out in a July 2015 visit to the Federal Correctional Institution in El Reno, Oklahoma that "the United States accounts for five percent of the world's population. We account for twenty-five percent of the world's inmates." 2 The Washington Post reports that the U.S. has built more jails and prisons that colleges, with more than 5,000 combined in all 50 states in the U.S. 3

There are as many answers to the question as there are opinions. The explanations (once researched) are absolutely endless. Here is a brief overview as to why we have such a high rate of incarceration (according to Mr. Waldman citing the Bureau of Justice Statistics, the U.S. incarcerates far more of its own citizens than any country (industrialized or not) in the world. (Indiana ranks 18th in the world ranking, far ahead of Cuba, Rwanda and Russia per 100,000 citizens). :

- War on Drugs; the 1990's saw a 'get tough' stance on drugs and sentencing which saw many inmates being sentenced to lengthy sentences. California and about half of the States had a '3 strikes and you're out' rule with mandatory sentencing for any three crimes committed. This occurred even while there was a simultaneous decline in the crime rate. 4
- Engrained racism; there is a stark over-representation of African-Americans in today's prison system. Although African-Americans make up just 13% of our total population they made up 38% of the total state prison population in 2011. 5
- Proclivity toward violence; in a very thorough analysis in motherjones.com, Mark Follman, Gavin Aronsen and Deanna Pan give us a clear idea of just one aspect of violence in America, namely mass shootings, i.e. these stats do NOT include crime and violence created by gang activity, armed

robbery or domestic violence. A 'mass shooting' is defined as a lone shooter taking the lives of at least four people (with the exception of the Columbine and Westside Middle School shootings which involved two shooters) in a public place. Since 1982, there have been 72 mass shootings across 31 of the 50 U.S. States (35 of these mass shootings have occurred since 2006 and 7 of them in 2012 alone). More than half of the killings occurred in a school or workplace with the other 30 occurring in shopping malls, government or religious buildings. 44 of the killers were white men (only one was a woman) who were mentally troubled, many showing signs prior to the killings. Of the 143 guns possessed by the killers, more than 75% were obtained legally. [6]

- Drug issues and incarceration for Veterans; as we discussed earlier, war and drugs have a devastating impact on the soldiers fighting the wars. In our most recent history, our country has been fighting a continual war in Afghanistan and Iraq since 2003-04. Ignoring (once again) the political ramifications of this issue, the reality is that many returning veterans have issues related to their time in Afghanistan and Iraq, such as PTSD or serious physical injuries which require pain management. Many of them attempt to adjust to life back home with the help of drugs (many times prescribed to them to deal with pain management and the psychological issues during their deployment) and alcohol, which oftentimes leads to conflict, arrests and incarceration. Countless of our veterans sit in county jail with no help whatsoever. Why? Because our county jails are not equipped or are overwhelmed by the numbers of veterans with dual-diagnoses.

Our Social and Environmental Degradation

I am by no means prone to hyperbole, never being accused (at least to my face) of exaggerating a problem, attempting to grow it into a crisis for my own purposes and manipulations. I do not mean to sound apocalyptic but as I sit here and write down these words, I can no longer ignore the feeling within my mind. I can no longer ignore this feeling: I believe that indeed our society (and by this I mean global society) is breaking down and this degradation is no longer on an isolated basis, rather it is on a global scale. I can go on and on about the environmental degradation (of which I am a firm believer in human-induced climate change) or the broken moral compass of our age or the outlandish growth in our technology and our inability to keep this growth in check or...on and on I could go. But that would be purposeless, wouldn't it? It would not propel us forward even an inch. What we need is something different, a different approach.

Regardless of the answers we might find of a rugged and robust individualism (Nietzsche or Rand) or a reboot of the collective communal social structure of socialism (Marx and Engels), we cannot help but begin with one, agreed-upon point from any and all sides: we are a broken world. We are 7+ billion people all clamoring for safety and reassurance that our side will be taken care of, all the while the floods on the coastlines are beginning and the chaos is rumored to be just over the hill...let's look at the etymology of the word *apocalypse*. It is from the ancient Greek and does not mean what we think it means (assuming you are a fan of any of the zombie apocalypse movies, as I am). It quite literally means *'an uncovering'* of a hidden knowledge, bringing to light earthly meaning to heavenly secrets. It does not mean a "destruction" or the end as we have interpreted it. It means that something is about to be uncovered, revealed to us as individuals, as a community, as a society and as a world.

Deflation in the 'church'

I grew up in the United Methodist Church (although my formative and most productive years in ministry have been within the far more civil, loving and less competitive United Church of Christ and Christian Church (Disciples of Christ). I was, however raised with a healthy dose of Wesleyan Theology which beautifully combines the Social Gospel with a truly evangelical approach to ministry. In short, I grew up believing that when applied with passion and integrity, the Gospel of Jesus Christ can change the world, literally. I was taught that Christianity had an element of science in it, in that if certain attitudes of the minds were combined with certain physical and social activities then God's Kingdom was nearer than before...John Wesley was and still is a huge influence upon my theology, which has a stringent work-ethic and a genuinely positive outlook on the world. I credit John Wesley and my father-minister Jack B. Haskins with planting the seeds of a jail ministry in my mind long ago as I listened to my father's impassioned and eloquent sermons at First United Methodist Church in downtown Shelbyville, Indiana circa 1978 or 1979. Imprinted upon my heart is this idea that outreach could change the way you see the world, change the way the church sees its mission and change the way the world sees itself and ultimately build the Spirit of Christ, bringing truth and justice and peace to our world.

It is within this theological context that I came to the ministry of LAM. When I speak apocalyptically, I do so with this idea that it is a revelation leading to a hidden, heavenly knowledge and understanding, not the end of the world. This is an important distinction to make, don't you think? Even in my darkest moments, I don't think the world is ending. We are however at a real turning point and I believe that we are entering this new era of revelation in our world and the church in particular needs to be about the listening and the subsequent understanding of this revelation. In order to do this listening and understanding we must first find a place of rock bottom, a place of deflation where we can meet and say enough is enough...let's start over.

I want to propose something, a new revelation upon which our broken world, our sick society can begin to build itself back up. *I want to propose that the best practical place to begin replenishing our society's collective spiritual energy is in the place where every community in America collects all of its most broken, violent, disturbed and desperate people: the county jail.* I believe that this is a fact for the rural counties as well as the urban counties, as we saw with the Vera Institute study. Every community in America has a county jail. It is the place to start for the faith community and Social Workers to begin building this new hope out of the lives of the community's most broken people.

Our community hit rock-bottom

One of the reasons LAM has lasted for over a decade in Knox County is because our community hit the condition of deflation or rock-bottom. By the time LAM had its beginnings in 2005, so many people and their friends and loved ones were being impacted by drugs and alcohol that we decided to do something, anything. It is still such a problem that we continue have support from the Knox County Sheriff, the County Council, Prosecutor Dirk Carnahan and the faith community and its approximately 95 churches within our 550 square miles of Knox County. This prevalence of the problem is why our annual fundraising banquet pulls close to 600 people in attendance each year and 1/3 of all the churches, not because we are such good organizers. LOL...no. The reason LAM still exists is because the problem still exists. The citizens of our county want to offer hope to those who need it and want it and our elected leaders have responded to this desire.

Does Incarceration Impact Drug Use?

I believe that just as an addict has to hit a point of deflation, a community must also hit rock bottom before it can begin to find relief. One of the key issues in hitting this point of deflation or rock bottom is that of decisiveness. A decision must be made. The last book of the Bible has a well-known passage which brings this point clearly to bear. John writes,

> I know your works; you are neither cold nor hot. I wish that you were either cold or hot. So, because you are lukewarm, and neither cold or hot, I am about to spit you out of my mouth….Listen! I am standing at the door, knocking; if you hear my voice and open the door, I will come in to you and eat with you, and you with me. (Revelation 3:15-16, 20)

I believe this is one of the most powerful passages within all of Scripture because it is so cosmic and so practical at the exact same time. It is speaking volumes to me here, primarily about the importance of a person or a community of people making a firm decision and moving into the future under that decisiveness.

Each community (whether it is led by its faith community or not) needs to realize that its first order of business within its own community is to decide to tend to those most in need. It is a racist waste of time to have a discussion of who is an American and who is not. It is my contention that every community can at least agree upon the fact that their county jail contains those who are most violent and most vulnerable and most lost. I believe that a community must decide to begin looking within the jail and sorting out those within the jail setting who are at a point of deflation, at rock bottom and help get them out of this condition. A decision must be made to collectively reach within that jail and offer a hand. A community must take ownership of its own problems. If a community wants to call itself a "Christian community" then it needs to stop playing identity politics and it needs to start practicing what it preaches, i.e. get in that jail and minister to the inmates who are begging for help.

You cannot wait for the state or Federal government to swoop in with a new policy or program to save the day. No offense to government programs (LAM was sustained early on with 4 straight years of a RSAT (Residential Substance Abuse Treatment) grants from the State of Indiana which received block grant funding from the Federal Government) but a community must take ownership of this problem. I believe that a community's ability to recover from a drug problem will be in direct proportion to its acceptance of its own problem and its willingness to financially support the solution.

One of LAM strengths was the uncompromising combination of approaches from social work as well as Christian ministry. Within the context of social work there is a decision to either have a macro or a micro approach. In the macro-approach the assistance is to the general environment so that a population/people could adapt and heal, improving for all involved. In the micro-approach the assistance is to the individual people within a certain population so that they can fit into their environment. 7 At LAM the approach was on the micro-level, with the idea that by healing the underserved people within this population then the overall environment is healed. LAM worked in the county jail because the addicts were an underserved group within our local population, this being termed the 'person-in-environment' perspective. 8

The historical connection of jail ministry and social work goes all the way back to 18th Century Britain with an English Sheriff by the name of John Howard and a woman named Elizabeth Fry. In the 1740's they began to notice the acute deprivation which prisoners experienced and began to give them attention. Their methods were adopted in the 19th Century in New York, Maryland and Massachusetts with a man named John Augustus beginning the first Probation Program in Boston in 1841 as inmates with alcohol-related charges were released into his care. Parole was introduced in 1884 as a conditional release prior to the completion of a sentence. 9 Therefore LAM is carrying on a rich tradition within social work of being in the jail as an issue of social justice within the framework of Judeo-Christian values. LAM was originally started by combining the original ministry with a homelessness task-force I was a member of back in 2004-05.

In terms of social work and the treatment of 'Alcohol and Other Drugs' or 'AOD,' there are three (3) primary methods of treatment: The first is to treat addiction as a moral issue and provide religious teaching and groups such as Bible Studies, etc. The second method is to treat it as a disease and apply a medical model with treatment groups along with medication for withdrawals and anxiety and depression as a method of treatment. The third method is the biopsychosocial method where each individual person is treated separately with the biological emphasis (physical illness issues), the psychological emphasis (depression and anxiety, etc) and the social emphasis (family systems issues, employment and community reintegration, etc.) LAM focused solely on this biopsychosocial area. 10 It is this emphasis on the biopsychosocial that made it unique.

The Question

Life After Meth, Inc. began with the question: how does a community deal with a drug crisis? What do you do? Where do you start? The initial answer is: begin with the faith community.

The faith-community is defined as: *the churches, synagogues and organizations of all faiths that espouse a message of love and tolerance and discipline among their active members.* Our faith-community is predominantly Christian, therefore we espouse a belief (albeit very general in nature) in the life, death and resurrection of Jesus of Nazareth as the beginning and ending of our faith with the clear message that a life of faith in Jesus will lead to a healing of our past. This healing of our past will lead to a new life where one can realize one's purpose and therefore reach toward fulfilling one's destiny. Yet addiction is such a brutal disease that one must physically survive it first then tend to the soul.

Higher Power

Every possible solution needs to be applied to this crisis in a person's life, including the 12 Step Program. This is why the 12 Step Program uses the controversial phrase "higher power" instead of the term "God" because a person must approach this subject honestly and openly. The truth is that many, many people are angry with God, resentful and bitter over feelings of abandonment and rejection. Many addicts and alcoholics have trouble even saying the word "God" for many years, having to approach God as a prodigal, inching their way toward their creator with different images and names before they can have a true relationship worthy of the term "Father" or "Mother." Ministry should never force an addict into a certain theological direction. Each addict and alcoholic needs to approach their higher power with fear and trembling. Indeed, we all need to seek our own relationship with God and stop looking at how another's path is wrong or sinful or 'liberal' or demonic. A seeker of God is a precious gift to our world. They need to be treated with care, not judgment.

When it comes right down to it, this recovery for the addict is a spiritual journey. It is a process of 'becoming.' It is no different for a family, a community, a country or for the world. It is all a process of becoming, of transforming, of re-birth. Christ speaks of being born again, being born from above. This being born again is sometimes a painful and laborious process, asking much sacrifice from us. There Is no quick answer. There is no quick fix for the addict nor for your community. It takes dedication to be born again, courage and perseverance, stubbornness and joy as well as a good sense of humor.

Let me introduce you to one of our LAM participants. Her name is Carly C. She is a 30 year old recovering meth addict and meth cook and mother of three beautiful children. By all appearances you would think she was your typical soccer mom (she does drive a mini-van) but she isn't. Her story is truly amazing and inspiring. I asked her what part her faith in God played in her recovery. She wrote this to me in an October 22, 2015 e-mail:

> My faith in God has played a huge part in my recovery. LAM is a faith based program which brought me into a more intimate relationship with Jesus. I know that for many years I was angry with God thinking the bad things that had happened in my life were his fault. I was broken and shattered which the Bible tells us in Luke 19:10 Jesus came to seek and to save [the] lost. And I was lost and needed [to be] saved. I was for sure not living for the Lord in my addiction and knew that he was the way, the truth and the life and after all the wrong I had done he was still there for me, just like we do with our children saying to them, 'it's ok, I forgive you and I love you.' The least I can do for the Grace I have received is offer my life to him and live for Him!

An addict must be changed from the inside out. As Jesus says in Luke 11:39, one must clean the inside of the cup first. 11 This cleaning the inside of the cup is a big deal. This strongly suggests that Christianity (indeed any spiritual awakening, for that matter) is much more psychological in nature than it is moral. In other words, true transformation (the type which I am sure you would agree Jesus is speaking of) is more than just "imitating right, moral behavior." Anyone can imitate behavior. True transformation is inward, rising from within a person so that they are not wearing it from the outside like a garment. It comes from *within* them, i.e. it is a psychological issue. This amazing insight of Christ can not only be applied to human beings, but also to families *and* communities: cleaning from the inside first.

Therefore our definition of ministry is: **_surrounding_** *people with the spiritual and physical support which allows them to discover their purpose and achieve their destiny.* Any faith-community (regardless of its religious theology or heritage) which espouses these same principles of faith, hope and love is a welcome partner in this journey of healing. In this respect ministry must always be based on the comradery which occurs when humanity and creation are nurtured in growth toward their potential. This is what is meant by ecumenical ministry. Politics should have no part in true ministry. None. A community must come together in a unified effort to tackle this issue of addiction. This means utilizing all of the means from:

- law enforcement community
- business community
- faith-based community
- social work community
- local government
- criminal justice/courts
- educational community

The Evangelical Objection to the 12 Steps

LAM attempted to create a new community of recovering addicts in our community. In doing so we create a 'beachhead' or a 'social safe zone' where recovering addicts and alcoholics can go as they begin or continue their recovery. LAM gives people SPACE to **heal** and **grow** and then **go** out and live their life to its fullest. We started this space within the confines of our local county jail. Why the county jail? Because it is the place where you meet addicts at their rock-bottom; i.e. you have their attention. Let's me share with you another insight from an email from Carly C:

Jail offers you no other way to turn and I feel that [when I was] shattered and broken and had burnt every bridge we meet people there in the jail who help build us up and help us grow. They love us until we can love ourselves. You have to want it [recovery] and work for it...and when you have so much time on your hands it gives you that opportunity to study and learn the tools that you need to make it outside the walls.

I have had many, many discussions with individuals over the years (addicts in recovery, well-meaning pastors, concerned parents, etc.) regarding the issue of disease versus faith. The main issue always comes back to the impact of one's faith upon an addiction. Many Christians believe that if you have enough faith then you will be set free from addiction. Many Christians believe that if you seek treatment (such as a 12 Step Program) it means that you don't have adequate faith in God to heal you. This is dangerous territory.

I believe completely that God can and does heal many addicts from this disease. I have no doubt that God does heal. Yet, I also have seen many, many addicts get "jail-house Jesus" and jump full-force into their faith, Bible-reading and church attendance as if their life depended upon it. They treat God in a dysfunctional way, as if God were another drug, trying to manipulate that feeling they get from the Holy Spirit just as they did meth and pot and pills and heroin. It is as if the Spirit of God is suddenly turned into a product, one which can be manipulated and used, like magic.

Christianity isn't magic.

It is much more complex and beautiful than magic. Faith, healing, and redemption sometimes takes a lifetime to receive. Salvation is not a product that makes you feel as 'high' as you did while you were on drugs. Healing cannot be manipulated. God is not a drug.

Drugs and alcohol (essentially) are an imitation of God. They imitate that sense of re-union with God which only God can bring (the word 'religion' means literally "to re-link"). Drugs and alcohol try and fill that God-shaped hole that is within us all. And they do for a while. The 1,400% increase in dopamine which meth opens up in a person's mind gives that person a sense of peace, power and invincibility which only a self-actualized individual (to use Maslow's terms) can truly attain. Drugs *take* that feeling of the "peace which passeth all understanding" and manipulates it. As P.D. Ouspensky says, narcotics don't add anything spiritual to anyone at all. It can only manipulate what is already "spiritual" in a person.

Life as a real human being is lived in *relationship* with God and God's created world. Life is not here to be taken and manipulated. This manipulation of God can lead to a dangerous result if one is not healed instantly of the desire to quit drugs and booze: if you are not cured from the addiction then it is YOUR lack of faith which is the culprit. If you still want to use drugs and drink then it must be YOUR fault, not God's fault.

This personal moral 'failure' just adds to the mounting guilt and shame and can and often does result in pushing the addict further from God instead of toward God. After even a few years of full-blown addiction, an addict has gathered up a huge amount of guilt and shame. They don't need any more guilt and shame.

Let me say this: I believe God can heal anything, including drug and alcohol addiction. I never say to anyone that EVERYONE must work a 12 Step Program and address this as a disease. I believe in getting better, in healing the person and the family and therefore the community by any ethically sound and morally responsible means possible. However, I have seen many people NOT be 'healed' instantly. This 'delay' in the expected outcome creates problems between that addict and their God. God becomes just another person who wasn't there for them. God becomes just another person who turned their back on them. God becomes something that God isn't.

Robin Amis and the Royal Road

In the early years 2000 (at the turn of the century) I made three trips to southern England to study early church prayer practices with a fascinating Englishman by the name of Robin Amis. At the funeral of my mentor Charles Ashanin in March 2000 I was put in contact with Mr. Amis, who invited me to study at some of his weekly conferences at his country estate near Devonshire (near Stonehenge). It was here (while still serving as pastor of Salem UCC) that I traveled three times to learn more about a subject which had fascinated me since my childhood: prayer. I knew about prayer...having grown up in the church I knew what prayer was...but I knew that there was something more.

What I learned in England altered the course of my life. I learned about a Christian version of meditation which has been lost to our modern, pietistic form of Western Christianity. Mr. Amis had studied for years about this early Christian prayer practice and had traveled dozens of times to several monasteries at Mount Athos in Greece, where he was considered a fellow worker by the monks at two particular monasteries. It was through his influence and teaching that I learned about these early, ancient practices and began to apply them to my life on a daily basis. What occurred in my life was nothing short of a miracle as I was led through a very dark time in my life: my divorce from Desiree when my son was only 18 months old. It was during this dark time that I remained as the pastor in Westphalia and started my LAM ministry in the middle of my trips to England.

When I entered the jail ministry in the fall of 2007 I began to apply these practices in some of the classes to the inmates. Meditation, in particular Christian meditation when combined with proper 12 Step work creates a dynamic energy which is miraculous in nature. I have seen the combination of the meditation and the introspection and confession of one's past allow someone to move past the stunted growth which an addict is 'stuck in' in terms of arrested development. I have witnessed grown men who act like they are teenagers begin to grow into adults, into grown men and begin to understand their role in society and in their children's lives and in the life of the community. I have seen meditation and proper Step Work heal a broken psyche. I have witnessed it and I believe this is one of the missing pieces of the puzzle regarding a truly effective drug rehabilitation program: meditation combined with 12 Step Work. It was one of my joys to connect some of the LAM participants with books about meditation and Christian spirituality and the Early Church Fathers.

Robin Amis wrote an amazing book entitled "A Different Christianity." In this book which defined his own purpose and destiny on this planet, he describes how early Christianity had engrained in its DNA a method of spiritual development which centered on the development of the emotional center. Christianity (to the early church) was therefore more about human psychology and not (as our modern pietistic Christianity sees it) about morality or the imitation of right moral behavior. It was about changing the mind (the psyche) and developing *conscience.* Robin writes, "The problem is that this therapeutic tradition has been suppressed as a result of the pietism and moralism that dominate modern Christianity. These tendencies to *externalize* the faith exist in all churches and all faiths. They are characteristic not of one religion but of a particular type of human immaturity: they belong to the lower stages of spiritual life, when people are using only one of the functions of their psychological life-they are driven by the senses and by what has been formed within us through the senses. But this practical method creates a true or spiritual morality by developing *conscience."*

How?

The real question is 'how?' How does a community of believers and non-believers focus their energy and enthusiasm on a drug crisis so that an addict can recover from their addiction and reenter their community? How do they focus their Christ-centered outreach and ethical-driven outreach so that permanent change occurs among those addicts and alcoholics they are serving?

We have all seen the various attempts at addressing this issue with 'conservative' churches utilizing a 'Jesus only' approach with a healthy dose of abstinence, Bible study and church attendance, while the 'liberal' churches utilizing a 'scientific approach' of applying programming, programming and more programming which includes medication, social work case management and a variety of support group attendance. In other words there are many, many ways to do this type of ministry. There is no single way to do this. I can only tell you our story and with humility say that there are other ways which work just as well. We, I do not have THE answer for you, for your family or for your community. However, we did DO SOMETHING about it, and lives have been changed, marriages mended and families restored and our community has been restored one addict at a time.

All I can do is tell you about my own experience in our own community.

The Early Days

As I realized what needed to be done (at least the theological reasons) I began to look around at the next course of action. My father was a retired United Methodist pastor at a nearby country church. The year before (2004) a woman named Rita Bowlin had asked my father if she could organize a community-wide meeting to address the issues surrounding the methamphetamine 'epidemic' which had just begun to plow through the Knox County community. They had a successful meeting, attended by local pastors, ministers, concerned citizens and those in the small group of recovering addicts. It was successful yet there was no follow-up.

A year later I followed-up, duplicating the meeting at my church in Westphalia on May 1, 2005. It was also a success with 60-70 in attendance. Many stayed afterward to discuss what could be done since there was such an acute need to do something. Several people in recovery and especially family members of current addicts stayed and spoke of the need to do something NOW. This wasn't just any other addiction. This was quickly taking people and families where they hadn't been before: violence, crime, unemployment and abuse could soon set-in within a few weeks of the first use. No one had seen anything like methamphetamine. It was such a quicker, self-destructive drug when compared to alcohol or pot.

There was such an emotional reaction to our initial meeting that I realized we needed to meet again, soon. It was obvious that the people who attended and especially those who stayed afterward wanted to do something, not just talk about it. We needed action.

We met in the living room of the church parsonage (in the same spot where Brent had sought refuge a few weeks earlier) and decided to form a committee with officers. We decided to plan a fundraiser at the Knox County Fairgrounds in Bicknell.

A Series of Fateful Meetings

In the fall of 2004 I was asked to sit on a newly formed Knox County Homeless Taskforce, which consisted of social workers and ministers. What a huge deal being asked to be on this committee would prove to be in my life! We met on a monthly basis at Community United Methodist Church in Vincennes. My first meeting to attend was on September 28 and the minutes from the meeting indicate the purpose of the taskforce. There were four areas of discussion:

1.) "short-term help: gas, food, overnight lodging, medicine, utilities"
2.) "transitional housing: emergency housing, short-term"
3.) "drug addiction/rehabilitation"
4.) "mental illness"

One of the main goals listed in the minutes from that first meeting I attended was the issue of housing; i.e. resources from other agencies, churches, purchase of property, criteria for use, 501c3 status, etc. Yet these goals were too broad. We had several leading social workers, pastors and business leaders sitting on this committee. (I was there representing the North Knox area) We would meet monthly, talking about the huge issue of homelessness and what we could do to address these needs in our community. We had good intentions but we had no focus, btw...good intentions without focus is just a waste of talent and precious energy.

At the May 23 meeting (the first meeting since our first LAM meeting on May 1st) I remember sitting there and thinking to myself that this taskforce had no focus. The general issue of homelessness was too broad and we were 'spinning our wheels." I suddenly had an idea: our two committees should merge! I waited for the next lull in the conversation and I spoke up, made my case that the new LAM committee should merge with this Homeless Taskforce and we should focus our attention on drug-related homelessness. In a dramatic turn everyone at the committee meeting agreed and voted that this should be so. In one swoop LAM had gained an amazing new source of energy, focus and influential members. We had grown tremendously in one dramatic moment. It was a turning point.

I have the minutes and the notes from that fateful meeting on May 23 and it is filled with ideas popping out of nowhere regarding resources and ideas for ministry including plans for a women's support group, looking into local pieces of property for housing, meeting with the Vincennes Ministerial Association at their next meeting, talking with the local newspaper and general ideas of focus being "dental/medical (holistic)/psychological." It is clear that there was a special type of energy which we had then, a synchronicity which we tapped into which suddenly brought several of us together with an intense focus on one specific problem.

In the meantime LAM's fledgling committee had continued to meet on a weekly basis with plans for our first fundraiser: a hog roast on September 17 at the Knox County Fairgrounds in Bicknell. Interestingly, some of the ideas for programming were as follows (as written in the May 7, 2005 minutes from Secretary Kim Hughes):

1.) "Pet Port volunteering with animals, possibly buy some land and build kennels to take care of those pets that would be put to sleep"
2.) "nursing home visits"
3.) "woodworking, sewing, different crafts"

At the May 16 meeting we elected officers and began to talk seriously about our mission statement. What were our goals?

By the June 7 LAM Board meeting we had begun to have focus. Our mission statement was:

"As members of the Body of Christ in Knox County, Indiana, we recognize the isolating and destructive power of Methamphetamine. It is our mission to work with respect, diligence and love with recovering Methamphetamine addicts toward their goal of [h]olistic recovery of body, mind and soul."

We had short term goals which included obtaining not-for-profit status, establishing guideline for our Board of Directors, starting a bank account, reaching out and including any interested church within the county as well as the long term goals of housing and obtaining grants to sustain our new program.

By the June 14th meeting we had a Board of Directors chosen (with 12 members) as well as a legal counsel from Mark Ewing who would help with filing the 501c3 status (which we had completed and approved by the IRS by October 11, 2005, thanks to Mr. Ewing). We had our first official LAM Board of Directors meeting on June 28, 2005 with Mark Ewing present, giving us direction regarding the formation of our 501c3 organization with by-laws, resident agent, goals, fundraiser plans as well as a dissolution plan.

I began to advertise for the September 17 fundraiser by appearing on WAOV's Knox County Today radio program. I also spoke at the League of Women Voters sponsored discussion of the drug crisis at Lincoln High School in Vincennes. The meth crisis was hitting the news more and more and there was talk of what to do. There was a panel discussion which I participated in, along with Sheriff Steve Luce. After the meeting Sheriff Luce approached me and said he was interested in teaming up with LAM and offering some drug-rehab classes to some of his inmates at the Knox County Jail in downtown Vincennes. A member of the newly formed LAM Board was a new friend of mine named Jay Carlson. He was the pastor of St. Paul's Lutheran Church (ELCA) which was situated two blocks from the Knox County Jail. We decided to meet with a group of inmates from Sheriff Luce's Inmate Workforce at St. Paul's on Monday nights for a couple of hours. (Knox County Sheriff's Inmate Workforce did manual labor and odd-jobs around Knox County) We would have a meal for them and guest speakers and topics of discussion such as Anger Management, Celebrate Recovery, etc. We began meeting with several speakers including Anne Hecht, Tina Hidde, Terry Jenkins and Rev. Brent Cramer to name a few.

Our LAM Board began to meet on a monthly basis and talk of focus was key. The Monday night LAM meetings at St. Paul's Lutheran Church were important but we needed focus. There was talk of assistance with dental care, 12 Step connection as well as the original issue of housing. At our October 17 Board meeting we had another crucial turning point. Sheriff Steve Luce (Knox County Sheriff since 2002) was our guest speaker. He brought a few representatives from his Inmate Workforce. As reported by Secretary Faye Bilskie, Sheriff Luce said that he is "looking to partner with an organization in regard to services. Incarceration is not the answer to the inmate's problems." Sheriff Luce wanted LAM to start up a half-way house for the inmates coming out of his Inmate Workforce Program and the Monday night LAM meeting at St. Paul's. The LAM Board agreed at the meeting to open a men's LAM House, with LAM assisting with job search, Activities of Daily Living (ADL) and assistance in programming. Thanks to a very generous and compassionate landlord named Pat Carter we were able to open the house. We would end up having the house open for 6 months, working with three men. One of those men was named Jody Smith. LAM assisted him with job placement and housing and he has enjoyed full time employment at Vincennes University ever since (as well as former LAM Board membership) and states that the LAM House was the key to his getting on his feet after being incarcerated in the Knox County Jail.

The original LAM House closed after 6 months due to the lack of tenants and the selling of the property by the landowner. We just had no real program other than the Monday night meetings at St. Paul's Lutheran in order to feed. We needed a focus. We needed a program. We were wasting our time and energy because we had not focus.

Days Wandering the Knox County Desert

For the next two years our organization attempted to do something about the drug problem in our community yet without a program and a supporting organization it was hopeless. We already had a tremendous amount of public support, particularly from the faith community. We attempted a partnership with the fledgling Bicknell Ministerial Association with a downtown building we had hoped would turn into a drop-in center but that did not work. We had a LAM Board Retreat on November 12, 2005 with discussion of developing a new position for a 'Life Coach,' but that did not work. We spoke of having a workshop with different community leaders, but that did not work. We spoke of starting a new women's group with Rev. Kate Lambertson from St. John's UCC which did meet for several months. Yet all of these issues (including the short-term LAM House) all had the same issue: no central program to use as a source of addicts to assist. It sounds odd that there was such a huge problem yet we could not reach those in need.

Mr. Michael Carney and the old Cemetery

The early (2005-2006) financial leadership was thankfully done by a very compassionate and professional banker named P.R. Sweeney. P.R. was our organization's first treasurer. He had been in banking his entire professional life and was well known in the community as a man of integrity. P.R. happened to be the chairman of the board of a 501c3 headquartered in Vincennes which worked people with disabilities. KCARC (Knox County Association for Retarded Citizens) had been in the business of assisting those with disabilities since 1972 and was the local, statewide and national leader in supplying those with disabilities and their families with opportunities at housing and employment. Mike Carney had started

KCARC out of nothing and had grown it into one of the largest employers in Knox County with close to 400 employees (both those with disabilities and those without). Mr. Carney is a businessman at heart with a compassion towards those members of society who are underserved, in particular he has been an outspoken advocate for people with disabilities for close to half a century. When I met Mr. Carney I knew that LAM and KCARC would be a perfect fit of social work and ministry.

Mr. Sweeney approached Mike about this little 501c3 called LAM that he had begun helping and he told him about its struggle to find direction. Mike decided to take a look and traveled to the little town of Westphalia where I still resided with my son Dylan. Back in those good old days when cell phones were just coming into their own, oftentimes the reception on the phone was sketchy and one had to roam around searching for a signal. Living out in the middle of northern Knox County was no different, so when I was on the cell phone that meant I was walking around a lot. The best place for a signal up at the Church was in the open ground throughout their ancient German cemetery. One warm winter afternoon I was meandering through the oldest section of the cemetery speaking on the phone and I spotted a man walking toward me. I quickly concluded my phone call since the man approached me with intent and excitement. His name was Mike Carney and he introduced himself, saying that he wanted to meet with me and discuss some issues regarding the possible cooperation between our two organizations.

I remember meeting with him at the Wendy's next to KCARC's Administration Offices (called Plant 5) and he proposed that KCARC become the 'parent' organization for LAM, giving it financial guidance and assistance with office space and general guidance from another not-for-profit which started out of nothing. He spoke of his belief that LAM needed an official director and that he felt that I was that person. I remember thinking to myself, "great, but we don't have any funds to finance a full-time position. Is this where my ministry is leading me? Is this part of my personal purpose in life? Is drug-rehab ministry a part of my destiny?"

Much of LAM's success was due in large part to the guidance of Mike Carney as well as the guidance from the administrative leadership of KCARC itself, under the leadership of Judith Kotter. Judith is really an unsung leader (and personal hero of mine) of LAM's ministry. I say this because she (along with her assistant Shari Shanklin) administered the financial branch of our program. They made sure our budgets were ready each year, they balanced our finances each month in preparation for our monthly meetings and prepared for our yearly audit. The financial credibility of your organization is a key component in your success. You need good people around you giving you sound service and advice like Judith and Shari.

The Cosmic Element

That initial meeting in the cemetery (and the subsequent meeting at Wendy's) would be another monumental meeting which would carry LAM to another level. Mike Carney's influence was enormous to the growth of LAM. He gave me the mentor I needed to teach me how to direct a 501c3. I was completely unprepared and naïve, yet I was teachable. His method was very Socratic as he did not tell you the answer to a particular question, rather he asked you questions, allowing the answer to rise up out of you. He is an extremely practical man, driven by an astute business mind. LAM would never have gotten very far if it hadn't been for Mike Carney.

In 2005 Robin Amis told me that "there is deep nobility in true service to humanity." Indeed that is what LAM does, that is what any true ministry does: it serves the needs of people. True ministry is: useful and unselfish and colorblind and fearless and choosy in its battles. True ministry connects to the people it serves so that THEY can realize their true purpose in life and realize their destiny. Period. These are not just activities that feed the body and keep it clothed and fed and warm. Those ministries are key, but true ministry goes beyond meeting the physical needs. True ministry looks to the eternal questions beyond time and space, acknowledging that there is another world beyond this physical one in which we live and breathe and suffer and laugh. There is a realm beyond this one.

The people we serve in LAM, the people we try so desperately to get off drugs and alcohol...they have a purpose in life and a destiny to realize. God has a plan for them, far beyond the trite and shallow bumper-sticker theology of our day. God has a cosmic plan for them and their children and their grandchildren. Looking for God's guidance in our ministry as we work with each and every person, this is our job (even those addicts who relapse and seemingly reject the message of the 12 Steps). Without this cosmic view then ministry creeps down into social work or Christian extremism. Ministry must have this cosmic element to it or it is just self-serving work.

Continued Wanderings

Mike began to meet with our LAM Board and give us direction. I began working on a few grants in my spare time at Salem and one in particular was submitted in the summer of 2006 (that would be crucial to our future). We continued to work on different ideas for LAM outreach with legal advocacy given by our great attorney friend named Jonathan Feavel. We had a Family Support meeting led by Pastors Faye Bilskie and Bill Talbott. Anne Hecht was working toward working with Foster Parents for meth babies. We had an idea about a scholarship fund for those in the LAM Program for the local churches to become involved in. We began to work with a local dentist named Dr. Doyle Ellis from Community United Methodist Church providing ½ price on dental assistance for those with meth mouth and general dental needs (which was an ongoing problem for many, many addicts).

By the August 14, 2006 LAM Board meeting I had stepped down as the President of the Board, making the motion that Rev. Bill Talbott become the President. The grant which I had written to the Indiana Criminal Justice Institute (ICJI) was denied in August and I could see no future for me at LAM. Even with all of the support from KCARC and Mike Carney and all of the church support, I felt that I needed to focus on my ministry in Westphalia and the raising of my son Dylan. I remained on the LAM Board and continued to attend the meetings. I even proposed an idea on March 31, 2007 for a LAM Film Festival highlighting success stories from the recovery community. We had great intentions but we continued to have no real direction at all.

The goal which I had in the early days of LAM was this: we needed to create a new community of recovering addicts within Knox County. We needed to find a program which fit this goal. We needed to start a new community of recovering addicts. But how?! The direction we were heading in 2005 and 2006 was leading us nowhere. We were directionless. It looked as if this would be just another good idea that died because of a lack of direction and support. We needed a break.

A Most Significant Day

In life one has a few turning points, times where (in hindsight) you can see a visible crossroads where you could have experienced defeat or victory with equal swiftness and completeness. These moments are (thankfully) few and far between because life is not so much lived under such circumstances. One such crossroads came for me in January of 2007.

I had been in Westphalia since January of 2002 and had been a single dad since the summer of 2003. I had one goal in life: protect my son and raise him in as calm an environment as possible (given the obvious pitfalls and dangers of a 'broken' home). Thankfully my relationship with my ex-wife was very smooth as we both maintained our respect for one another as well as the mutual realization that Dylan's well-being was paramount to both of us. (Life seems to be all about choices, doesn't it?)

Dylan would be starting kindergarten in the fall of 2007. My ex-wife Desiree and I had 'joint-custody' of Dylan. She had remarried and had moved to nearby Vincennes and wanted to place Dylan in the public school system in Vincennes. Westphalia was 30 minutes away and I realized that in the best interests of my son I needed to move to Vincennes and commit to a new life there, dedicating my energy to the continued raising of my son. I recall being on the phone with my mother in January of 2007 and saying "Mom, you know what I really want to do? I really want to quit and move to Vincennes and be close to Dylan." Right then (as happened so often in my life, my mother helped me talk through one of these big moments in my life) I knew what I needed to do.

I had a brilliant plan: I was going to quit my job and move to Vincennes without any job waiting for me. Brilliant. I would completely make a leap of faith, go full Kierkegaard and jump without a net. Brilliant. I would do it and not look back. Brilliant.

I told just a few people as I began to make plans to move to Vincennes and decided to tell my congregation at Salem in early May of 2007. The Monday after I resigned (my church contract stated I needed to stay an additional 90 days after I officially resigned) my pastor friend Jay Carlson and I were invited by Sheriff Steve Luce to tour the new jail (which would be completed in July of 2007). I remember coming around a corner in the new administration section of the Knox County Jail where they had some empty cubicles set up. He paused and said, "This is where your office is going to be."

I said, "What do you mean?"

He said, "Your LAM office. I have found a program for us to use and I want LAM to run it. I want you to be the Director of the drug rehab program here at the Knox County Jail.

LAM Executive Meeting: May 8, 2007

On May 8, 2007 the Executive Committee of the LAM Board of Directors met at the new Knox County Jail. The minutes submitted by Faye Bilskie state the following:

> Sheriff Luce discussed working with LAM. He felt the connection between the Sheriff's Department and LAM would bring a spiritual faith as well as motivation through programs to the inmates. He felt the new jail would be the perfect home for LAM. He felt this to be a working combination for the inmates whose lives are "on pause." Programs would keep the offenders focused on their recovery and reentry into the community

The minutes state that Sheriff Luce recommended that I be appointed as the new LAM Director and I should start at 2-4 hours per week, working on grants to fund the program. The minutes also speak of a new program which Sheriff Luce had introduced me to: the Community Model Program from another 501c3 called The Center For Therapeutic Justice headquartered in Emporia, Virginia. The Center For Therapeutic Justice was founded and directed by Morgan Moss and Penny Patton. They knew a man named Delbert Boone who would be coming for his first visit on June 6. A prayer breakfast was scheduled for July 19 at the new jail to introduce the faith community to the new program.

The minutes from the May 21, 2007 LAM Board meeting indicate a new beginning as the Knox County Jail Commander John Vendes and KCARC's Director Mike Carney joined the LAM Board of Directors. At the June 4 LAM board meeting it was agreed that I would be a part-time Director of LAM for $1,000 per month for a maximum of six months (because at that point LAM would run out of funds). Beginning on August 1st I had 6 months to investigate and apply a program for the jail as well as write a grant to continue funding. So basically we needed to have found firm footing by Christmas, no big deal.

The 2007-2008 LAM Board officers were as follows:

- President-Rev. Andy Kinsey
- Vice President-Rev. Jay Carlson
- Treasurer- Keith Carter
- Co-Treasure-PR Sweeney
- Secretary-Faye Bilskie
- Co-Secretary-Peter Haskins

The Trip to Emporia, Virginia

On August 20-22, 2007 Sheriff Luce, Mike Carney and I flew down to the Southside Regional Jail in southcentral Virginia to a town called Emporia. This facility (more the size of a small prison) was the home of the best example (in the U.S.) of a Community Model Program and we were visiting to see if we wanted this program in our county jail.

Sheriff Luce and I had already met the Mr. Moss and Ms. Patton and had a pretty good idea that we wanted this program for the LAM Program. Yet it didn't take more than five minutes inside the Southside

Regional Jail to convince me that this was what we needed back in Indiana.

By the September LAM Board meeting we had made the decision to sign an agreement with The Center For Therapeutic Justice (referred to as CFTJ from now on). The LAM Board agreed to compensate CFTJ for their services and training as we all worked together in setting up a Community Model Program at the Knox County Jail. An employee of CFTJ named Carrie Williams would start programming at the jail on November 6, with a salary going to her, to CFTJ as well as to me. LAM, Sheriff Luce and the faith community had made a commitment to the success of this program. We were going for it.

The Community Model versus the Therapeutic Model

In addition to the visit Sheriff Luce and Mike Carney and I made to the Southside Jail in August of 2007, I made an additional trip back to the program by myself on August 4-7 of 2008. I made extensive notes during both my visits, which serve as a testimony to the strength and power of witnessing the program in action.

Firstly let me distinguish between the two general types of drug rehabilitation programs available to the incarcerated:

1) Therapeutic Community Program: this is where you have staff who teach the classes to the participants. This staff is usually trained social workers or certified drug rehabilitation counselors who teach the classes in a typical classroom setting.
2) Community Model Program: this is where the participants themselves teach the classes, utilizing their own life

experiences to create a new community of recovering addicts within the jail or prison setting.

This idea of a community model is nothing new but it is an amazing idea (and as PD Ouspensky wrote, "Ideas are machines of great power.").

Moss and Patton were so very evangelical (if I can use that term in a secular reference?) with their enthusiasm for the idea of 'therapeutic justice.' They were a fascinating and vibrant couple in their early sixties who had worked diligently at spreading this idea of therapeutic justice. They were fascinating and loving hippies who were determined to get the 'good news' out about this new way of looking at a local jail setting.

"Therapeutic Justice means that any involvement, and all contact with the criminal justice system, would offer an opportunity for education, healing, and restoration for the victim, the offender, the community, and the criminal justice staff. Therefore, Therapeutic Justice means working together to increase respect, usefulness, and safety in an area of human experience that has all too often been characterized by pain, neglect, and frustration....Therapeutic Justice means communities reassume the responsibility for satisfying justice and correctional systems become known as human service centers." 13

This is what we needed! We needed a program which addressed our chief and only desire for LAM: to create a new community of recovering addicts within Knox County. The place to do this: inside the county jail! The local county jail would be the place to begin the building of this new community. It all seemed so clear to me. I knew we had finally found a focus to our social work/ministry: the county jail. It would all start in the county jail!

LAM was struggling with reaching to addicts themselves. Now we would go into the jail and reach out to them and create this new community within the jail. The ramifications were endless and exciting on a social, economic and employment, family, housing and spiritual level.

As we sat and observed the Community Model Program in action at the Southside Jail, I furiously took notes. I noticed how there was order and respect and civilized behavior within this jail setting. I was fascinated with what I was witnessing. The best way to communicate this with you is to share with you my own report to the September LAM Board upon our return to Vincennes:

> The environment in the Community Model Pod is one of discipline and support. The inmates have been organized in such a way as to have their entire day modeled after a typical work day. After an hour of personal preparation and reflection they all gather in a circle where they begin with a morning roll call, followed by everyone expressing their feelings. They then have a morning meditation with unlimited commentary on the reading. The rest of the day is structured around specific classes and videos on the 12 Step Program, anger management, parenting, spirituality, family issues, etc. Staff has very little to do with the teaching. The inmates are trained and become the speakers for the vast majority of the groups. They have key community meetings throughout the week to keep the community organized and flowing smoothly.

> The community is structured around a very democratic process with three to five members being voted in by the community as "senior members." These senior members are the ones who maintain the order of the community. The new members apply and (if accepted) are given a 2-3 week trial period. Remaining in the community depends on the member following a strict set of rules, in addition to the jail rules and the participant contract. If any rule violated there are automatic consequences.

> There is also a time when each person is given a chance to give a push-up (encouragement) and a pull-up (ways to improve)

to an individual or the community. There is always a milieu of respect and encouragement to anyone who desires to work on recovery. For those who are negative, disobedient of any rules or disruptive they are asked to leave the community for 30 days (after the third removal they are no longer welcome back in the community).

The Community Model Pod we observed created an environment of discipline and support for those interested in working on their recovery. The atmosphere was amazing in its concern for the individual, yet placed the burden squarely on the individual to admit their condition, rely on their higher power and begin taking a moral inventory of their life. This structure is developed so that when they are released they will have these new habits of recovery set-up in their life. These inmates are people of amazing talent whose lives have been put on hold. LAM's mission should be to give them a chance to start over. We need to provide the framework and guidance. It is up to them to make it work in their life.

October 31, 2007

I remember it well: Halloween night of 2007. Penny Patton, Morgan Moss and I spent several evening hours interviewing Knox County Jail male inmates. (we decided to begin with the men first and then progress into the female inmates soon) We went from pod to pod and eventually visited all seven pods, looking for what Morgan called "ringers." A ringer was an inmate who was 'sick and tired of being sick and tired.' It was someone who was broken down by their disease and ready to give up and seek treatment. It is the only way to truly get help: you must be broken. It is what the 12 Step movement called 'hitting rock bottom.' The original idea came from Bill W.'s influential friend named Ebby H. who had sought out the help of none other than Dr. Carl Jung. Dr. Jung described this 'rock bottom' in terms of being 'deflated.' 14 One must be emptied psychologically and physically, realizing that there is a stark choice to be made between life and death. It is here at this point that an addict begins recovery because they have to, not because they want to. There is a difference.

We were looking for the people who were deflated. It is a tough call and this was my first crack at it. I was coming at it from a completely different angle than a corrections officer or a social worker. At the time I was coming at it from a pastor's angle which means this: just listen to them and be genuine. In other words a pastor should first and foremost be as open-minded as possible. Judgement and defining a person is not the initial role of a pastor as they sit down to listen to someone in crisis. A pastor needs to listen. I would learn very quickly how to remain in that place yet also begin to discern the tell-tale signs of manipulation and lies.

I would learn that a local jail setting is a dangerous place for the naïve. It is filled with expert liars, manipulators and criminals who are just getting started in their life of crime and drug use. In other words a county jail in the United States of the early 21st Century is generally (and I use this term very, very loosely) filled with four types of criminals:

1) **Novices**; those who have not been in the system long enough to be sent off to prison for long periods of time. These are generally people who are young, who have grown up in a rough social environment and who are very comfortable in the jail setting, i.e. the people in the jail are people from their own socio-economic background, their own neighborhood and oftentimes their own immediate and extended family. Jail is a social-setting for them, it is a family-reunion. There are very few 'ringers' in this bunch.

2) **Revolving doors**; those who are former novices but who have graduated up into the professional tier of the local criminal

scene. These are generally men and women in their thirties and forties who have spent their adult life under 'the installment plan' (as Morgan Moss used to say). In other words they have spent time in and out of jail AND prison and are very comfortable being taken care of by the county: three meals a day, a warm place to sleep and no responsibilities. These are just boys and girls who are suffering from 'arrested development,' i.e. they have the body of an adult but the maturity of a teenager or child (they act the age of the date of their drug-onset). There are very few 'ringers' in this bunch.

3) **Rock-bottom boys (and girls);** those who are not criminally-minded but who are suffering from the disease of addiction. These are generally men and women over the age of thirty who have children and who have spent time in and out of jail and prison. In other words, these inmates are just addicts, not criminals. They can also be first-timers in the jail who have had a long history of addiction in their life but who have only now reached rock-bottom. These are the people who are served best by a drug rehab program in a county jail because jail is serving as a 'wake-up call' for them. Jail is a terrifying experience as they realize where their addiction has landed them: isolated and on the road to destruction. There are many, many 'ringers' in this bunch.

4) **Pathological Criminals;** to meet a true, professional criminal is a rare occurrence, thankfully. Working in a county-jail setting I have met very few of people I would categorize as professional criminals, but they are there in our society. We hear about them in the news. They are truly pathological in their thinking, with no sense of right and wrong, empathy or compassion toward other human beings or toward creation. Many in this category come across as very compassionate and loving yet there is something sinister which is within them. For LAM's ministry in Knox County, this type of incarcerated

person is beyond our help. This is why we have jails: to sort these people out and get them off to prison. One of LAM's biggest job is to help sort out the low-level criminals and drug addicts from the pathological criminals who need to be held accountable for their actions. The true criminal is no one to be taken lightly, this is serious business. This is why I was thankful for Sheriff Luce and Sheriff Morris and their professional staff who are trained to deal with these types of inmates. It is important to rely on the training and wisdom of local law enforcement, especially doing this type of ministry. Remember: you are not here to save everyone, just those who truly want to change.

On Halloween night Morgan and Penny and I gathered up the names of men who professed that they had indeed hit rock bottom. The next day we turned in these names to Sheriff Luce and he instructed his jail staff to assist us in moving 12 inmates to their own section of the jail (B pod) where they would begin forming their own recovery community within the confines of the Knox County Jail. This was the beginning of our mission: to assist addicts in recovering from their addiction and to assist them in reentering our community. It took two years, but we had arrived at a program.

The Community Model Program

In an article the January/February 2006 edition of *American Jails,* Morgan Moss and Penny Patton offer a "paradigm shift in jail programming." 15 This paradigm shifted consisted in the application of a proven evidence-based program (EBP) (i.e. the Community Model Program) in the local jail setting. Moss and Patton write,

...jails are going to have to do some things differently in response to the call for jail accountability, results, and a value-added product to society, not just custody housing. Most jails are under pressure to do more with less. Here is one alternative. The CM [community model] approach offers an opportunity to make a shift and "take the fork" that increases public safety, reduces societal costs, and serves large numbers. **Today your jail is the most critical intervention society has to stop the revolving door to prison and to stop family and community violence while saving taxpayers money.** [emphasis their's] 16

Several of the main points of emphasis which Mr. Moss and Ms. Patton made with us as they spoke to the LAM Board and Sheriff Luce were:

1) The CM creates a 'civilized' environment within the jail setting which reduces the safety issues for the jail staff.
2) The CM is 'cost-effective' in that it utilizes the inmates themselves as the teachers instead of costly staffing costs.
3) The CM creates a natural 'bridge' between the jail and society before the inmates reach prison, saving the state and Federal governments in costs of incarceration.
4) The CM also creates a living community within the confines of a jail setting (applying social learning/recovery model/whole systems/experiential/ cognitive restructuring theories within that setting) 17

The more I read and listened to Morgan and Penny the more I realized this was a perfect match for me and for LAM. It was a professional and spiritual approach to social architecture. I recall being invited by Morgan and Penny to come and listen to the Dali Lama at an appearance in Bloomington, Indiana on the Saturday prior to our first LAM interviews (October 27th). I remember what a beautiful autumn day it was in Bloomington as I went to hear one of the greatest spiritual leaders of our time speak with eloquence and tranquility about the true nature of civilized life. It all begins on a personal and therefore a psychological level.

All the problems of our time can only be addressed if one takes personal responsibility for the search for a solution. My cosmic job had now transformed into making a little corner of my little world a better place, one person at a time...one person at a time, from the inside out. This focus on the inward orientation was music to my ears and I ran with it...all the way to jail.

Details, details, it's all in the details...

From November 1, 2007 until April 4, 2009 Carrie Williams was officially in charge of the day to day administration of LAM's Community Model at the Knox County Jail. As the agreement between CFTJ and LAM was solidified and progress forward was made at the jail, it was my job to sit in on as many meetings and classes as possible and learn from Carrie. I even visited another CM at the Monroe County Jail (which was administered by an organization called 'New Leaf/New Life') in Bloomington, Indiana. My job was to learn as much as I could, all the while drumming up support in our Knox County community and churches as well as set-up support groups and coordinate employment assistance with Vocational Rehabilitation and KCARC's Dove Employment Services. I also made one more trip (this time a solo trip) back to Emporia, Virginia and the Southside Regional Jail to learn as much as I could from a fully-functioning CM Program. In all of these visits and observations I learned several key factors which contribute to a healthy CM Program;

   1) *Structure*: if there is a one word summation of the Community Model it is 'structure.' The program gives the structure for the community to come together and begin to make decisions based on a very democratic concept of governing. Implicit in this is a great deal of trust in the process of wisely selecting those who are 'deflated' and ready for change. In other

words, you can't just place a bunch of convicts in a pod and give them rules and curriculum and expect them to form a functioning community. It takes discernment on the part of the staff and team leaders to choose wisely.

2) *Accountability:* there was a set of rules which the community writes and amends which dictate the automatic consequences of any violation. If there are any violations of these rules then a participant is subject to the consequences. Below is a complete sample of the rules:

Sample Program Rules:

1) *Respect all jail rules and jail staff::*
   - Be quiet after lights out, being loud during quiet time is boardable (1 noise check)
   - Do not look at the females.
2) Respect All Groups:
   - be seated by the start of group, no eating during group
   - stay seated unless you are called by a guard
   - no sleeping, head down on table. You are expected to participate in all groups. If the class is an elective then you can work on your step work
   - be in a circle so everyone can see you
   - be fully dressed in jail uniform
   - no non-program material during groups (books, mail, newspapers)

3) Respect all other community members' space and property- and the right to not be subjected to boisterous behavior

4) Any issue arising from violation of any of the rules shall be brought to a community vote.
   - Do not use the board for non-class things, such as drawing, threatening to take someone to the board, etc.
   - If you say you are going to take someone to the board then do it! This "false threat" is a boardable issue.
5) Violation of any of the following is automatic removal from the Program:

   - Physical violence or threats of any kind,

149

sexist or Racist comments, breaking anonymity, stealing. *Any use of illegal drugs or alcohol is automatic removal from the program as well as additional charges from the Sheriff's Department.*

6) Team leaders are appointed by the Director at his/her discretion. Team leaders are trusted servants of the community. They do not govern, the community self-governs! Any person has just as much authority as anyone else.
7) Negativity is not tolerated!
8) Disrespect and provocation are not tolerated!
9) Anonymity; breaking of community/individual anonymity is automatic removal. Anonymity is very important. What happens in the group stays in the group, no matter how trivial the issue. Nothing leaves the group:
   - If you are a sponsor, what is said between you and your sponsee stays between the two of you.
10) Unkempt beds/cleanliness:

   - You must have your beds made (to the satisfaction of th Director) and uniform on by 8:30 each weekday morning.
   - Do not hang towels, washcloths, clothes on the rail.
   - *All members will participate in the monthly cleaning of the pod/space (the last Friday of each month). Refusal to fully participate will result in removal. Subject to the satisfaction of Sheriff, staff and Program Director.*
11) Tobacco chewing:

   - No chewing in class
     * No smoking; *If you are caught smoking (a violation of a jail rule) you must teach a one hour class on a book (chosen by staff) within one week.*
12) Homework:

   - You must have your homework finished by due date (as established by facilitator and co-facilitator). Homework not turned in by due date is a boardable offense.
   - Homework assignment must be written on the board by the facilitator, otherwise it is not regarded as homework.
13) Prayer Time (8:30-9:00):

   - You are to be dressed, have your bed made, etc. by 8:30. Every member is to report to opening circle by 8:30 a.m., even if you are sick. You will inform community that you are taking a sick day and then return to bed.

- The purpose of prayer time is for prayer/meditation, counseling with another member. It is meant to be a calm lead-in to the day ahead. You may not play cards, watch t.v., etc.

14)Removal:

- If you are removed or remove yourself you will be re-interviewed in 30 days.

- If you are removed or removed yourself from the community you will be subject to an automatic search of your belongings to make sure no unauthorized (per Director) material leaved the pod.

15)*Books/materials; each participant is allowed up to three recovery-related books (in addition to a Recovery Bible) to have in their possession. Each participant will have a folder, a pencil, an eraser, 15 pages of loose leaf paper, a journal, a Recovery Bible and a copy of the rules.*

16)Resource Man:

- Every 6 weeks the community will vote for a new resource man who is responsible for supplying books, paper, packets, etc. Abuse of power will result in new appointment of resource man.

17) 12 Step rule:

- You must work the 12 Step Program to the best of your ability. Step 1 is not optional.

18) *Recovery House: to be eligible for the Recovery House a participant must be in the jail program at lease 90 days and in good standing with Sheriff Morris, jail staff and the staff. He must also be interviewed by the Director and the House Manager at the County Jail prior to final approval.*

19) *Participants will be subject to random drug screens (supplied by the Program).*

20) *Each person who is interviewed for entry in the Program needs to be a resident of the jail at least 30 days before they are eligible.*

21) *Each person who is interviewed by the staff and team leaders will only be accepted after final approval by the Sheriff.*

3) *Spiritual Awakening:* this is the third item I gleaned from the CM Program at the Southside Regional Jail: the inner life. It all boils down to spiritual awakening for me. The disease of addiction is an opportunity. It is an opportunity to awaken to God's purpose in your life and to move toward realizing your destiny. The 12 Steps are the perfect program (EBP) to utilize for this awakening. The type of intense suffering which addiction brings can bring about an equally intense amount of spiritual awakening. As Charles Ashanin said, "When you suffer know that God has begun to answer your prayers." A participant named Rasheese W. in the CM at Southside said during his class on Step 4 (taught on August 21, 2007), "I can fool you...you all...but I can't fool my higher power." A recovery without the acknowledgement of one's higher power is no recovery at all.

LAM Program 2007-2015

The LAM Program had its growing pains. Indeed. (It has been shut-down briefly in February of 2008 by Sheriff Luce and another time from March to July of 2015 by Sheriff Morris due to drugs entering into the program...relapses happen anywhere at anytime) Carrie Williams and CFTJ remained connected with LAM until the early Spring of 2009. It was at this point the Mr. Moss and Ms. Patton decided to sever ties with LAM due to the independent and faith-based nature of our organization. In other words, we were much more faith-based in our approach to the Community Model with more of an emphasis on creating a sustained community of recovering addicts supported by the faith-community as opposed to maintaining a strict Community Model. We were much more interested in having a self-sustaining community of recovering addicts than we were a model Community Model, if that makes any sense?

Let me give you an example:

If one were doing a strict Community Model Program you would have no one else teaching the classes except for the participants themselves. Yet I was interested in bringing in different pastors and lay leaders from the Knox County community to teach Bible Study classes or to just sit-in on some classes. I was also interested in teaching some classes on spiritual development and the prayer life as well as having Professor Jesse Coomer come in the jail and teach classes on creative writing. We wanted to do this in order to connect the participants with churches and our wider community so that when they were released they had familiar faces waiting for them. I wanted to offer a wide variety of subjects in order to give our participants opportunities to 'test the waters' in areas that they may never have even considered. I remember one participant in particular named Chris M. who was interested in Professor Coomer's class on writing. Chris joined our group as we began to write some short stories. Chris began to write a suspense novel and would bring it to the classroom and read us each new chapter. This 23 year old was amazing!!! He was a fantastic writer and we encouraged him to continue. He was sent to IDOC (which means he could not take any of his writing with him to prison) so I kept his writing for him. When he was released from prison I mailed him his novel and have never heard back from him. I hope and pray that Chris has continued his writing.

It was our proclivity to make the Community Model fit our local needs which caused us to sever ties with CFTJ. So, on April 4, 2009 I officially took over as the only employee of LAM, running the jail program in addition to the re-entry program. The learning curve was steep.

Let me confess one thing: I had no business doing what I was doing. I was not a recovering addict or alcoholic and I had never directed a non-profit organization. Apparently the only prerequisite for this ministry

153

is the naïve belief that it should be done because there were people in need who were suffering.

Sheriff Mike Morris

In the midst of this departure of the CFTJ, we also had the resignation of Sheriff Steve Luce in January of 2009. It was in the middle of his second elected term as Sheriff of Knox County and he decided to become the Director of the Indiana Sheriff's Association located in Indianapolis, Indiana. He resigned in February and the precinct chairpersons elected long-time road officer and veteran of the Knox County Sheriff's Department Major Michael P. Morris. It was obvious from the start that Sheriff Morris would continue to support LAM and its ministry at the Knox County Jail.

It cannot be overstated how important Mike Morris was to our program. As Delbert Boone pointed out early on in our discussions regarding the Community Model: the key to it all is that is starts ***locally in the county jail***. Working on a state or Federal level is much too political and it is easy to lose control of your narrative. The narrative is what drives your local mission, the mission to begin in the local jail. You must maintain control of your narrative.

The key to a successful program is all in the county jail and that begins and ends with the county sheriff. He or she is in complete control of that facility and has the power to say what kind (if any) of programming, church services, food, detergent, snacks, etc. come into that facility. To have Sheriff Morris continue the LAM Program at the Knox County Jail was a blessing for our ministry. Indeed in the early months of 2009, LAM was just getting started and we needed time to establish a new community of recovering addicts in the jail before we could create one in our community. We owe our gratitude to Sheriff Morris for allowing us to continue our ministry.

As I have said before, I am not a recovering addict or alcoholic and have never been arrested. I have had three speeding tickets, one ticket for not stopping at a stop sign and a seat belt ticket, but I have never had issues with law enforcement and have always had a great deal of respect for police officers and those in the military. Being involved in the LAM ministry has allowed me to be given the opportunity to be around law enforcement officers for the first time. Since 2007 (Tania and I shared an office at the Knox County Jail) I have been blessed to get to know several officers from the Vincennes Police Department but mostly from the Knox County Sheriff's Department. I have been so impressed by the comradery and professionalism I have witnessed among the jail staff as well as the Sheriff's road officers. These are the men and women who are on the front line of this drug battle being fought in our homes and schools and factories. These are the men and women who have to deal with the drunk drivers, the belligerent patron of the corner bar, the meth cook in the North End who is freaking out because he put too much lithium in his latest batch of meth, the burglar breaking into your house looking for prescription pills. These are the people we call on first when we are in trouble. These are the people we need in our communities, the people who really care about the welfare of the people they serve, who understand how very close our communities are to chaos and anarchy. I have gained a tremendous amount of respect for law enforcement while being given the opportunity to minister to the addicts at the Knox County Jail. Yet it all begins with your local sheriff and law enforcement officials. These relationships with local law enforcement need to be appreciated and cultivated by the churches if the mission field (which sits in your back yard) is going to be harvested.

Funding and Local Government Support

LAM (and any ministry or program which begins in the local jail setting) makes sense on several levels. To be sure, I am speaking from a minister's standpoint. But from the standpoint of county government it makes fiscal sense. If you look at the costs of housing an inmate in a county jail for one year it is obvious that each county jail in the U.S. needs some type of programming;

- $35 per day (the standard rate which Indiana Department of Corrections pays a county jail to house one of their inmates) X 365 days = $12,775 per inmate

It makes total sense to be working toward some program to divert some of the inmates away from a lifetime of incarceration. *It only takes a few inmates to easily pay for any type of ministry or program.* It was because of this idea which pointed LAM in the direction of gaining local government support for the sustaining funding and support of our program. I remember Delbert Boone saying that inmates in a jail setting should be looked upon not as criminals but as potential tax-payers. It is a win-win situation for a local community to work within their jail as a source of salvation for many but also as a source of revenue as well.

But an organization needs a "financial foothold" in order to gain traction and local sustaining support. Where do you start?

The following are bullet points of key points in our financial growth. Hopefully this will give you and your church/community some ideas applicable to your situation:

- **State Government**; for four years beginning in 2008 and ending in 2011 LAM received a Residential Substance Abuse Treatment (RSAT) grant through the

Indiana Criminal Justice Institute (ICJI) ranging from $100,000 in 2008 to roughly $49,000 the remaining three years. ICJI is a sister organization to the Indiana Department of Corrections headquartered in Indianapolis. Because of the influence of Moss and Patton and CFTJ and a similar grant in Monroe County (for 'New Leaf New Life') LAM received these grants to help support staff (the vast majority of grants do NOT fund and staff salary and support). Thankfully after four years we were able to sustain our ministry and did not need any ICJI support, yet that support from the Federal Government working through the State of Indiana was crucial to our early growth.

- **Local Community Foundation**; On February 14, 2008 LAM received a huge break when we were chosen to receive the first start-up grant from our local Knox County Community Foundation (KCCF) in what they called their TLC Grant for $50,000. A wonderful friend of mine named Kathy Rinsch was the new Director of the Foundation. She and her Board President (a compassionate attorney named Mark Ewing) proposed that LAM receive this grant. Mike Carney and I gave a presentation to their entire board and we received it, amazed at what was happening. From December 2007 to February 2008 LAM received two grants which gave us ample room to begin establishing our LAM Program in our local jail and community. It was an amazing chain of events which gave us such confidence and excitement.

- **Faith Community Support;** at a LAM Board meeting sometime in the summer of 2009, Rev. Dan Clemens suggested that LAM have an annual banquet as a fundraiser. On February 18, 2010 LAM had its first annual banquet (held at the First Baptist Church in Vincennes). We had 220 in attendance at the first banquet and raised enough funds to be very encouraged by our efforts. Our first three banquets were held at the First Baptist Church and then we moved to the Highland Woods Community Center in order to accommodate our growing crowd of community supporters. Each year we have LAM participants give their testimonies about the importance of the LAM Program in their recovery. Each year we have over a quarter of all the churches in Knox County (there are approximately 95 churches in Knox County alone) present at that banquet and they get to witness where their funds and support go: a local mission field right in their own backyard. The last year I was the Director (2018) we had 596 in attendance with 31 churches represented.

- **County Government;** at our first annual banquet we had all of the members of the Knox County Council in attendance. Led by Council President Tim Ellerman, Steve Thais, David Culp, Bob Lechner, Emily Heineke, Jim Beery and Mike Thompson invited us to make a presentation at a county council meeting on April 13, 2010. We asked for funding to help us begin a women's program and we received it. In 2012 and 2013 we asked for and received additional funding from the Knox County Council to assist us in establishing our transitional housing. The role of the Knox County Council (in particular Steve Thais, Jim Beery and Bob Lechner) cannot be overstated. Their support has been so encouraging as we have reached out into our community and attempted to create this new community of recovering addicts. During the final four years of my tenure as the Director we received $77,500 each year from our local County Council, with a total of well over $500,000. This is what I call a dedication by local leadership and this is what you need: local leadership to buy-into the idea that addicts are worth this investment on many, many levels.

Clear and Repeated Objective

If I remember anything about my early meetings with Mike Carney I remember how he would constantly say to me "LAM is only going to be successful if it is faith-based." He would drive home that point to me over and over. I heard him. I believed him. But it doesn't hit home until I look back and realize that an organization (any organization for that matter) is successful only *if they have a clear objective and they are consistently focusing and re-focusing their sites on that one objective. Remember? You must maintain control of your narrative.*

Our clear objective was this: our ministry is based on support from the churches and the faith-based community in Knox County. The church-support gave us the foundation to move out into our community as well as our state and find the support we needed for initial support as well as sustainable support. We started small and worked in the details and made sure we never lost sight of our faith-based roots. We were and are after all, a ministry first and foremost.

One of my most difficult hurdles doing LAM was the fundraising portion of it. In short: I hated it (and still hate it). Why? Because asking for money makes me very uncomfortable. Even as a pastor I seldom bring up the topic of tithing or money or fundraising. I was pressured several times by a particular person to turn LAM into a business. I always resisted.

This resistance was interpreted as meekness and weakness in the face of a challenge. LAM was to remain a ministry as long as I was around. How many ministries get caught up in this prosperity-gospel game? LAM was to remain a ministry, not a business.

Yet the early days of LAM saw many hurdles I needed to jump over as I attempted to apply the principles of Bill W.'s social architecture to our community. Make no mistake about it: if you are trying to do a jail/drug rehab ministry in your community you are doing social architecture. You are attempting to create a new community of recovering addicts within your larger, organic community. When you attempt such an undertaking you must understand something: you are going against years and years of engrained social behavior. For years and years our community as well as our society has dealt with alcoholism and drug addiction in strange ways. Many times it is dealt with through humor, simply ignoring the problem or mass incarceration (which is what our society began doing in the mid 1990's). No matter how our society or our community (s) has dealt with addictions, make no mistake, they dealt with them in some way. They have kept a social balance and many times it has created a very dysfunctional atmosphere. There are many, many odd and tragic aspects to our individual communities and families which are created in order to just move ahead and deal with difficult issues such as the disease of addiction. Oftentimes these attempts at dealing with them just lead to bigger problems. No matter how these issues are dealt with, it is very, very difficult to break through these social walls which have been built up. I saw some of these social walls which my Knox County community had built up, and I had to have a strategy.

In those early days of LAM, I had a series of very, very skeptical communities to win-over. In other words I had some convincing to do. I had to prove that I was for real. Here are just a few examples:

- *The 12 Step Recovery Community*: I am not a recovering alcoholic and/or drug addict. Period. This caused the 12 Step community (Alcoholics Anonymous and Narcotics Anonymous) to look upon my work with LAM with skepticism and doubt. I was accused a being in this "only for the money" or "only for a job." (Tradition Six states that "An A.A. group ought never endorse, finance, or lend the A.A. name to any related facility or outside enterprise, lest problems of money, property, and prestige divert us from our primary purpose.") I even had someone comment that I was not qualified to direct the jail program *because* I was not in recovery. I remember Delbert Boone was there and he said to me (I remember because I hurried to my desk and wrote it down), "Peter's alright. He knows this is strange. He's diggin' at it and that's what you need to do: dig at it." As LAM progressed I made sure the 12 Step community understood that LAM was utilizing the 12 Step Program as its primary source for its Evidence-Based Program (EBP) and nothing more. This allowed for our participants to have a recovery-community to join immediately upon their release to our community.

- *The Law Enforcement Community:* Working as a pastor within a jail setting can be difficult. Much of the skepticism that I heard was only in the first several years of LAM. However, Tania and I continued to hear this from time to time. Some jail officers felt that I was only doing this 'ministry' for the money and that I didn't really care. Besides, in the eyes of many jail officers, the population I was working with was nothing but a group of manipulating felons who are only trying to use me and our ministry to get of jail quicker. In doing LAM for several years now I realize why there are those in law enforcement who have a hard time believing an inmate when they are locked up and suddenly 'find Jesus.' The job of a law enforcement officer on any level is one thing: maintain peace and keep our community safe. They are not here to minister to people. The primary purpose of the local county jail is not to be a drug rehabilitation facility. It is a jail first and foremost. Yet our job at LAM (and any jail ministry) is to give those inmates (who are at rock bottom) a chance. It is indeed our job to believe them when no one else will. It is a VERY delicate balance because there is a limit to our patience as well. Sometimes we have to say 'no' to someone when we have given them chance after chance and move on to another person. But it is our role in the local jail to be those people who do indeed give some inmates a chance to say 'enough is enough.' This is why the role of the local Sheriff is so crucial in giving a ministry the opportunity to go into the Jail and offer people hope.

- *Social Work Community*: From 1997 until 2001 I work as a social worker in the field of mental health and the homeless who have a mental illness. I enjoyed working as a social worker (though not as a professional since I didn't have any undergraduate or graduate degree in Social Work). I enjoyed doing 'quiet' ministry (ministry without saying it out-loud). My experience doing case management as a social worker taught me so much about how to do the re-entry part of LAM. Yet doing LAM has taught me to appreciate the nature of ministry as opposed to social work: i.e. a minister doesn't 'clock out.' Oftentimes (not always) the typical workday of a social worker ends. There is a very distinct line between when they can 'help' someone and when they are 'off the clock.' Ministry does not do this (oftentimes to the detriment of the minister and their home life and social life and the high level of burnout). Yet it is the nature of ministry which says 'I am here for you at all times of the day or night.' If someone at one of our LAM Homes has a crisis at 5:05 p.m. on a Friday afternoon then I am going to be available. I would never say, 'call me on Monday morning.'

As I look back on these struggles I realize that I had two qualities or should I say 'conditions' which I put to good use: 1) stubbornness 2) naïvete. These two qualities led me far enough down the path so that after several years the 12 Step community, the law enforcement community as well as (but not to the same degree) the social work community have all seen that I am a person of integrity and LAM is an organization of integrity. When it all comes down to it, personal and collective integrity is all that you have.

LAM had one objective throughout its entire existence and this was our narrative: the creation of a new community of recovering addicts in Knox County. Over and over again I said...at churches, at Kiwanis, at Rotary, at County Council meetings, at Knox County Community meetings, at United Way meetings, at LAM graduations, in the jail, at the coffee house, at Wal-Mart...over and over again. LAM has had a consistent message throughout its existence and now we have examples of participants in recovery to show our community that this is what we are doing. We have proof. In terms of business integrity, LAM (with the help of KCARC and their administrative offices) consistently has clean fiscal audits year after year. We were proud of the fact that our ministry had this type of integrity. We had proof.

Tania Willis and the Women's Program

During the early days of LAM we had the desire to focus our ministry on men AND women. Alcoholic and drug-addicted women in this country are one of the most severely underserved populations. Initially we addressed this need by having the pastor from St. John's UCC in Vincennes start a weekly meeting for women, yet both the men's and women's ministry did not have a program to utilize as a source for the support groups or for the men's house we had in 2006 or for any portion of the LAM Program. We had to wait and develop the Community Model Program in the jail first before we could do anything. In other words, we had to start small and build it from the ground-up. When we started the program at the jail we started with the male population and this is why;

It is plain to me that in a county jail setting such as our community, there are many more men incarcerated than women. Many more. I can only speak specifically of our situation here in Knox County, but the jail population of men versus women is usually a 5 to 1 ratio. There are usually around 15-40 women incarcerated at the Knox county Jail at any given time. Because of this they are housed in one unit, called a 'pod.' There are just so many more men housed in a county jail. There are plenty of questions as to why this is so, but few answers. I believe one of the answers has to do with the presence of children.

In the surveys that we take at the beginning of each participant's time in the LAM Program we ask them several questions:

- One of the questions is: *"How old were you when you first began using drugs and/or alcohol?"* The average age for BOTH men and women is: **13 years old.**
- Another question is: *"How many biological children to you have?"* The average number of children for BOTH men and women is: **2 children** (this does not include

step-children or foster-children, only children born to them).

- Another telling question is simply: *"What is your age?"* The average age of the men in our jail program is: **31 years old.** The average age of the women in our jail program is: **35 years old.**

Interestingly, the answers for the first two questions for both the men and the women have the same average answer, yet the average age is older for the women. Therefore one could conclude that there is another reason why there are so many more men incarcerated than women. As I have eluded to, I believe that the answer is the presence of these (on average) 2 children. It is obvious that just as many women get involved in addictions at the same age as the men do. Yet the men are getting arrested at a much younger age AND at a much higher rate. It would seem that the presence of children in the lives of the addicted women are having an impact on when and how often the women are incarcerated. If there is a drug arrest oftentimes the father of the children will go to jail many more times before the mother will go to jail. This is done for practical custody issues by law enforcement, with law enforcement trying their best to maintain some order and structure for that particular (albeit dysfunctional) family. The father is incarcerated (an average of 7 incarcerations for the male LAM participants) multiple times and is essentially taken out of the role as caregiver for their children. The mother of the children continue to get deeper and deeper into their addiction and eventually law enforcement and the court system and probation must incarcerate the mother. A county judge can only give a mother so many chances with layer upon layer of probation sentences in a valiant attempt at 'waking her up to her responsibilities as a mother' before a jail sentence is handed down. And that is what Tania Willis sees as the LAM Female Program Facilitator: broken down mothers in their thirties and forties who have had 15-20 years of drug addiction and alcoholism. By the time they enter the LAM Program, the women are much more broken and hollowed out by their disease than the men.

The Knox County Council Helps Start the Women's Program

One of the most important pieces of wisdom I learned from doing LAM was this: start small and do it well. This was a knowledge passed on to me by the business-mind of Mike Carney, who tutored me in the ways of his world, the world of projects and planning and goals. He showed me how to apply this to the men's program in the jail. Now we would apply it to the women's program.

We started with the men's program at the Knox County Jail, mainly due to the fact that we were able to have many more inmates to choose from as well as space. Early on the men's program at the Knox County Jail was allowed to have our own space or pod. This was an essential part of the Community Model which Moss and Patton had taught me: LAM needs its own space in order to build the community of recovering addicts. This was one of the basic applications of the community model to a county jail setting. Sheriff Morris allowed the men's program to have its own pod. There was not enough space or female inmates for the women to have their own pod.

With the blessing of Sheriff Morris in early 2010 (a little over 2 years since the men's program was started) we were ready to start a women's program. Our first banquet was held on February 18th and by April 13 the Knox County Council had graciously approved monetary assistance for LAM to begin a women's program. I recall speaking to the Knox County Council and reporting to them that the current recidivism rate for the LAM men's program was 31%, compared to 64% for the general jail population at the Knox County Jail. The LAM Program cut the recidivism rate (the rate of return of an inmate within three years of release) in half. The savings to Knox County was significant if you took the Indiana Department of Corrections rate of $35 a day to house an inmate, which resulted in a cost per inmate of $12,775 to house one inmate. The program pays for itself very quickly.

By May 11, 2010 we hired D.W. to lead the women's program at the Knox County Jail. We had many growing pains during those first several months, including the use of space at the jail. Logistically, the LAM women had to utilize the classroom at the jail for their classes, whereas the men could stay in their pod and have class in their living quarters.

Many, many things go into building a community of recovering addicts within a jail setting:

- Trust in each other
- Anonymity
- Hope of change
- Faith in God
- Faith in themselves...

It is doubly difficult for the women because after their group sessions in the classroom they must return to the oftentimes toxic environment of the pod holding the general female jail population (which comprises those women who have said 'no' to LAM and a life of recovery...you do the math). It can be very, very difficult to create.

By November of 2010 it was clear that D.W. could no longer continue as the Female Program Facilitator for LAM. By January 11, 2011 we had hired Tania Willis (on a recommendation by our then LAM Board President Jane Melvin) to be our new Female Program Facilitator. Little did we know we had hired the perfect person to help take LAM to the next level. Tania and her husband David had just concluded a three year stint as missionaries to an orphanage in Honduras (through the General Baptist Church). She was not looking for a new type of mission work, but she found it: drug addicts in a county jail.

Tania had several characteristics which made her the perfect person for this job:

- Faith: she has a remarkable faith in the risen Christ who can literally heal anyone's past and lead them into a life of purpose and meaning.
- Dedication: she has the amazing characteristic of be very loyal and dedicated to those she ministers to and serves.
- Stubbornness: when she focuses in on a person to serve she is tenacious in solving the problem (s).
- Motherly: she is able to 'mother' or 'parent' the women in her program so that those motherly traits are awakened within them and they can then take their place as mother of their children.

Tania was the key to LAM growing and expanding for those reasons and more. If had not been for Jane Melvin introducing us to her back in 2011 I don't believe LAM would have been successful. She gave me and the program a non-anxious presence who was a person of immense character and integrity, all the while mixed with a stubbornness and tenacity, the likes of which I had never seen in ministry. She would go toe-to-toe with anyone and remain rooted in her belief that everyone deserved a chance at redemption. She is a dear friend and even though I have moved on from LAM I continue to consider her a fellow minister in our endeavor to serve the addicted in our community.

Hiring the right people is so vitally important to any job, but in particular a ministry. This goes without saying, yet it is so essential to ministry. If you are going to do effective and impactful ministry you must respect, admire and care for those you work *with, not just the people you work for*. I have had several poor experiences with supervising pastors (all of them male, by the way) who looked at me as a competitor instead of a partner in ministry. At times I wasn't even sure if we were serving the same God. It is so very damaging to any ministry when there is this type of competition within a staff. I would highly recommend patience, planning and discernment as your organization/church/community begins looking at hiring staff for your program. It can make or break your program.

Part III: Conversion

"*Conversion*, the third facet of the core A.A. idea, was a term avoided. Yet the profound reality of the concept was inescapable: "bottom" clearly implied that there was something else "higher." Most obviously, the conversion experience in Alcoholics Anonymous was from drinking to dryness. It was a turning from the condition of active alcoholism to a total life-style termed "sobriety.'

Ernest Kurtz, "Not-God" pg 34

This third part of my memoir is kind of a pep talk for you, your church, your family and/or your community if you would like to start something like LAM in your community. When I began I would have loved to have had someone or some guide to give me direction...and maybe there was a guide written out step by step to help me but I just was unaware of it...either way I want to utilize this chapter as a sort of '*how to*' section with several bullet-points which are clues as to the 'lay of the land.' I made many mistakes which were unnecessary so hopefully this will help you. [At the end of Part III you will find some questions for a small group from your community to begin talking about starting a drug rehab program in your local jail. Hopefully this will help.]

The idea of conversion which Professor Kurtz speaks of is a sticky wicket, isn't it? It is saturated with religiosity yet is a term and an idea which is inescapable when it comes to spirituality and to the 12 Steps themselves. One of the major caveats which I would point out is the inescapable conflict which a 12 Step/religious drug rehab program has with a local mental health provider which utilizes a medical model as their Evidence-Based Program or EBP. Although I am a former employee of Knox County's local mental health provider (Samaritan Center/Good Samaritan Hospital) for a brief time in the late 1990's, as the Director of LAM I was in constant competition and sometimes conflict with them regarding the basic premise of an effective drug rehabilitation program. Not to get into too many details, they relied on a medical model of addressing an addiction as a disease which needed to be treated, just as cancer or diabetes would be treated. Whereas our EBP was the 12 Step model (which is utilized in 80% of all drug rehab programs across the U.S., btw) which relied on those in recovery to guide others into recovery with an emphasis on four-sided approach of: self-evaluation, confession, restitution and giving back to the community as a framework for that recovery.

In a recent publication by Maia Szalavitz entitled *Unbroken Brain: A Revolutionary New Way of Understanding Addiction,* there is a wonderfully articulated view of this medical model. In a May 1, 2016 article on National Public Radio, Ms. Szalavitz gives a typically arrogant expression of this view, reducing the 12 Step Program to just another 'self-help' program. She believes that an addiction is a medical problem, indeed a disease (which is ironically one of the foundational breakthrough idea for Bill Wilson as he co-founded AA with Dr. Bob in 1934-35) and should be treated just like cancer or diabetes or Parkinson's or…She reduces the 12 Steps to moral and religious proselytizing, stigmatizing anyone who does not have these conversion experiences which Bill W. had in 1934 while in the hospital with Dr. Silkworth. She laments the history of AA in America as it has come to dominate the field of addictions. She argues that 70% of people drop out of the 12 Step Program within the first 6 months and when compared to other therapies such at cognitive behavioral and motivational enhancement therapy, the 12 Step program performs no better. She firmly believes that AA and drug treatment should "amicably" divorce, leaving treatment to those who are highly trained in the profession of drug-rehabilitation.

While I certainly do not concur with Ms. Szalavitz's views regarding the viability of the 12 Steps, I do understand her trepidation regarding the religiosity of the 12 Steps. One of the main groups of opposition I met in the early days of LAM were those of the Christian Religious Right. I remember fondly how I was accused of being "New Age" because I had spoken of the "Christ within" at a gathering of religious leaders. Throughout the early days of LAM I had to try and convince our community that an addiction was indeed a disease and NOT a moral failing, which is close to Ms. Szalavitz's argument *against* the 12 Steps (ironic, huh?) Therefore I am in no way advocating for the utilization of the 12 Steps as some sort of proselytizing tool for my/our religious fantasies or sick displacement of personal shortcomings.

The 12 Steps work for some people. The medical model works for some people. The 'Christ only' model works for some people. There is no program that works for everyone equally, so for anyone to say that a program that does indeed work for some has to be divorced from treatment is missing the point. The point is this: addictions and the way in which they have adversely impacted our country is a serious threat to our nation and its future. Any program should be used in order to try and help as many addicts as possible. I certainly always advocated for someone to go the 'Christ only' route if they chose or the medical model if they chose. I was never arrogant enough to think that the 12 Step Program or the LAM Program was the only program that worked. You have to have an Evidence-Based Program to work from (if you are truly interested in grant writing, that is...) and the 12 Step Program is the most widely utilized. But one should never think there is strictly one program that works. It is such a negative trait of Americans to think that we need "one" answer to a problem. There is no one answer or program or prayer or step to win this 'war on drugs.' It takes an entire community applying many remedies to alleviate the symptoms of the malady of addiction.

173

Further Outreach

As we said, the proof is in the pudding, right? If it works, it works. The key to any drug rehab program is to make a decision and go for it. The key point is you must begin to meet the needs of the addicts. This issue of meeting people's needs is a primary idea within drug rehabilitation. Until you meet people's basic needs they will NOT move toward self-actualization, salvation, sanctification or whatever word you use to describe it. Recovery is not just about physical survival. Recovery is about a person being able to reach their potential as a human being. In other words, until you feed and clothe and shelter people, they won't talk about their kids and their job and their relationship with God or their disbelief in God or their dreams in life. There is a saying in AA that you must save your 'ass' first before you can begin saving your soul.

The LAM board of directors began talking seriously about moving into transition housing in the summer of 2012. I vividly recall one of our respected community leaders trying to convince me to NOT move into the area of transition housing, telling me it would be a quagmire, full of endless drama, manipulation and ultimate failure and embarrassment of the LAM Program. I took in this advice, genuinely asking myself the question of 'why' we were moving into the area of housing. This issue was not a new one. From 2007 until mid-2013 we only had the jail program. One of the driving forces for me thinking long and hard about starting two transition homes was a very practical reason: clean people coming out of our jail had nowhere to go besides the drug houses. I cannot tell you how many times we were frustrated that many of our participants had no place to live when they returned to the 'streets.' Tania and I would sit in our office at the jail and try and come up with a plan to send them to nearby mission houses or bigger cities which had more to offer or somewhere. We were always frustrated because we did not have the option of housing. We had wanted housing for so long as an option to those who were serious about their recovery, now was our time.

Jody Smith and the Impact of Housing

Jody Smith is credited with being LAM's first success story. He is still clean and sober, working at VU. I see him on Sundays as he attends my church (First Christian Church) and we go to lunch quite often. It is wonderful to see him there, proof that this stuff works. He was in the first group of inmates involved in the LAM Program who were on Sheriff Luce's inmate work crew. We met him back in 2005 at St. Paul's Lutheran Church two blocks away from the old jail (when it was located across from the Knox County Courthouse). Little known fact: LAM had its first transition house before we had a jail program.

Jody was our first resident of our first LAM House. Although the first LAM House only lasted for six months, it was critical in Jody's recovery. He was on our LAM Board of Directors for a while back in 2012 and 2013 as we were making plans to open our transition homes. He told me once that the most important aspect of the LAM ministry in his life was the LAM House. He stated that having that place to go to *immediately* following incarceration was the key to his recovery. I had never heard Jody say that before. At that moment I knew that we had to open a women's home and a men's home as soon as possible.

Why? Why was the issue of housing so important to Jody and his recovery? I have two answers, the first is the intellectual answer and the second is the practical answer:

1.) **Maslow's answer**: we have already spoken of this before but it needs to be reiterated, namely that basic human needs must be addressed before any civilized behavior can be brought out of a person. Spirituality is a luxury. (Generally speaking) It is not sought when the belly is empty (unless we are speaking of unique, saintly human beings). Food, clothing, shelter need to be addressed first. (an aside: this is why many,

many families are relieved when their drug-addicted son or daughter is finally arrested and incarcerated, because then they know he or she is alive, fed, clothed and housed. Period. Housing is a big deal)

2.) **Burned bridges:** the real, practical, tangible reason that housing is so vital to an effective drug-rehabilitation program is the issue of burned bridges. Plainly spoken, (particularly for women) by the time you are arrested and incarcerated for any length of time you are deep into your addiction. (Delbert Boone told me once that for the first DUI charge that person had already driven under the influence of alcohol over 1000 times and not been caught) By the episode leading up to incarceration, the disease has literally 'eaten-up' relationships with those who love them most: family and friends. The last thing to go is often the job. When a person in addiction loses their job it is often the tipping point which signals the beginning of the end. They have now burned all of their 'bridges' so extensively with family, friends and vocation that their only people or group they have to turn to for ALL of their needs are... (yes, I said ALL of their needs) their 'friends' in the drug community. You see, the drug community has a social structure to it as well. It is often one based on violence and manipulation and is almost always based within poverty. When one speaks of poverty, one speaks of one common thread which runs through all of their social structure: loyalty. Those engrossed in the social structure of poverty are extremely loyal to one another. The drug culture is no different. Relationships within the drug community are oftentimes based on remaining loyal to one another. Therefore, whenever someone who is still in active addiction gets out of jail or prison and is in need of housing, of food, of shelter, they are ALWAYS welcome at the dope house. As long as they aren't snitching for the cops and as long as they are ready to join everyone on the couch as the foil is passed around then they will be taken care of just like they are a part of the family. In other words, if LAM did NOT provide an alternative to this sick sense of family and loyalty then almost all of the work we did in the jail program was for naught, for nothing, it was futile. We needed to provide an extension of our jail program. It was a natural and perfect fit, but not an easy task to say the least.

Indigent

Many, many inmates are released from jails and prisons and have absolutely nothing but the clothes on their back. In terms of a local jail, everyone exits the jail in the clothes which they wore when they were arrested and incarcerated. If they were arrested in July and they are released in January, then so be it. This directly addresses the homelessness issue which LAM grew out of back in 2004 and 2005. Homelessness is a tremendous issue for convicts as they are released from jails and prisons. When it all comes down to it, the only reason LAM has ever existed is to help those forgotten addicts and alcoholics who aren't getting the help they need to survive and thrive as human beings. My relationship with William H. was a wonderful example of this struggle to provide assistance. As I was discovering first hand, this assistance was not the usual 'band-aid' approach that most people, agencies and especially churches utilize. What I mean by this is most of our approaches to altruism or assisting those in need are limited to throwing a tremendous amount of resources and money at one particular person or cause for a very limited time and then moving on toward the next crisis. Americans (especially) have a proclivity toward 'throwing money' at a cause, a mission project or a person but not staying around long enough to help that person through the crisis situation. We don't stick around long enough to show them how to utilize these resources we are throwing at them. As a consequence we have many well-meaning people trying to help people in genuine need, but because we can't commit to those people for the long run, we waste our time and money and energy.

We need to learn (as I have learned) that the best altruism is based on patience and attention, not money and physical assistance. The money and the supplies to help a community recover from a hurricane or flood or an HIV outbreak are very needed. Only the naïve say that money isn't important. The physical needs are vital, yet they shouldn't come first. Long-lasting and effective altruism is based on the *quality* of the after-care which can be provided as well as the level of *integrity* which surrounds those who are providing that care.

Take William H. for example. In a letter from July of 2013 (months before his January 2, 2014 release from Plainfield Prison near Indianapolis) he opens his letter with this pleas,

> *Pete, Hello. How are you [?] I received your letter and it was a relief to know that I've still got someone in my corner, so to speak. I am anxious about my release date/CTP date approaching so quickly and being unprepared. I hope you can understand the gravity of my situation. Being released with no resources, nothing, no clothes, shoes, personal hygiene, nothing and the prospect of being paroled to E'ville [Evansville] homeless shelter in that indigent condition...scary...huh[?]...Fear, uncertainty, and feeling extremely "POWERLESS." Can you relate? I know I need to trust in God, and I do. I know He will provide. Also my children's situation, loving them so much. I've done my best to parent from in here [prison] and an occasional phone call and weekly letter helps. But "I'll be home soon" gets a little weak sounding sometimes. When they need me so badly.*

At the time of this letter we only had a women's transition house opened. We did not have a men's house open, i.e. I had NO place for William to go when he was released. I had to prepare a place for him. I had to make it happen. I had six months to open a men's house.

The process of opening two transition homes was much bigger and complicated than I had anticipated. It is an odd thing, because I knew that it would be difficult. Yet there is nothing like experiencing the working out of the details and walking through all of the engrained resistance within a community to teach you the true nature of your undertaking. I was learning how to think in terms of patience and attention. I was learning.

Tania Willis, Mike Carney and I traveled to three different transition facilities to have a tour, talk to the directors and staff and 'cherry pick' their ideas. We were honest with these three facilities and their staff that we were investigating and searching for ideas. We visited the Progress House and Agape House in Indianapolis as well as the Amethyst House in Bloomington, Indiana. We were given a copy of their house rules and began to get an idea of what we wanted for LAM. We examined their rules and methods of operation and chose the best way for us to proceed. We took many months in investigating and planning this move toward housing. We were still moving slowly and deliberately.

In addition to those three organizations, we had several local, key individuals who contributed to our housing program getting off the ground who need special recognition:

1) Anonymous donor; this generous individual donated seed money for us begin looking for the right location without having to be overwhelmed by the costs. It was because of this person's loving gift to our ministry that we were able to launch our new segment of our care.

2) Ben Singleton and the Anson Family Farms; Ben Singleton was on our Board of Directors and realized that we needed to have a leap of faith. Along with his family, they purchased a home in the heart of Vincennes and decided to rent the rooms to

179

our LAM participants (it is important to note that LAM does not own either one of our LAM Houses) with LAM providing the programming and case management. By May 31, 2013 all of the repairs, painting and preparing were finished as we opened our home to the female LAM participants. Kathy Borden was our first resident and house manager.

3) Jared Chattin; Jared and his father Rex are farmers in the North Knox area. Jared is also a long-time friend of mine as well as the pastor of Bruceville and Wheatland United Methodist Churches. He and Rex are two of the most gentle and loving people I have ever met. Whenever we started working on the housing project, I remembered that Jarod owned a home in Vincennes (approximately five blocks from the women's home). I approached him regarding the renting of it to our men's program, and Jarod saw this as an opportunity to extend his ministry. He graciously agreed, and we opened the men's house on October 9, 2013 with Steve Seale and Aaron Shotts as our first residents.

It was on May 31, 2013 that LAM opened a women's transition home in the heart of Vincennes. We had no reaction from the immediate neighborhood regarding the opening of a women's LAM House. Yet when we began to make progress toward opening a men's LAM House we started hearing very negative reactions from the immediate neighborhood. The rumors about the house and resentment toward our ministry began to build and build so we organized a community meeting on September 30th to give the neighbors a chance to express their views as well as give our ministry an opportunity to explain what we were going to do.

I recall that meeting as a very, very stressful episode in the life of the LAM ministry. There were thirty or forty neighbors there, almost all of them quite angry at our supposed maneuvering and manipulating our way into their neighborhood. We had several LAM Board members there along with the Mayor Joe Yochum and Vincennes Police Chief Dusty Lueking (to whom I will always be grateful for their support at that critical meeting). We met in the living room of this large, Victorian home (a former residence and doctor's office location in the heart of Vincennes). Tania and I decided to have only two LAM participants there as spokespersons for the 'cause.' Kathy Borden and Steve Seale will forever go down in 'Lam-lore history' as the two who calmly and eloquently defended the idea of a drug rehab house in the heart of Vincennes. I say it with a smile now, but on the night of September 30th it wasn't so funny.

Kathy and Steve brilliantly responded to all of the questions (whether or not they were kind-hearted or fair) with a dignity and class which to this day makes me smile with pride. To this day I understand the neighbor's fears and reluctance to have a bunch of felons living in their neighborhood. I understand that they feared having child abusers and sexual predators living in our LAM House (we do not allow sex-offenders into our program in the first place, let alone our LAM homes). They wanted reassurance that we would have adequate and substantial supervision of the facility, because they were already going to take a 'hit' on their property value. There was a lot of anger that night, but there was mostly fear. I get that. Steve and Kathy assured them that they ALREADY had drug houses in their neighborhood. The LAM House would be the one property which would be supervised so that it would be drug-free. We tried to reassure them that we meant what we said and we would supervise the residents. Yet when the meeting was over and we had all gone home I had realized that running a drug-rehab house was no walk in the park. Addiction and the recovery from addiction is a mean game, one best played with a humility and an empathy for the addict as well as the sober.

The Leaders of the Drug Community

Kathy and Steve were two of the biggest leaders of the drug community for many years. When Tania and I met them at the jail and invited them into the LAM Program we had no idea (really) the wisdom behind converting the leaders of the drug community first as a practical means of addressing the drug problem in a community. As I said before, the drug community is a social structure based largely on loyalty. Loyalty is the common thread which runs through the fabric of the drug community. There is loyalty to those who pay attention to you, who care for you and most importantly loyalty toward those who can and will consistently supply you with your drugs. There is a hierarchy within the drug community.

When you begin to create this new community of recovering addicts, it all starts with the conversion of the leaders of the drug community. If you can convert some of the drug dealers and the manufacturers to a clean and sober life filled with the normal responsibilities of civilized society then others will follow. To be sure this 'leadership gap' within the drug community will be filled by others who are not ready to quit their addictive lifestyle, but at least your community has gained something in the exchange. These former leaders of the drug community are now leaders of a new community of recovering addicts who are now given 'permission' to stay clean, pay their child support and taxes and keep a job and go to church with their kids. It is suddenly socially accepted to live a life of civilized behavior and before you know it something begins to happen in your community: healing begins to take place within families and within your community. But it all starts with this conversion of the **leaders** of the drug community.

The Talent

It is important to note that drug addicts and alcoholics are people with many, many talents and ambitions and amazing personality traits. Addicts and alcoholics are oftentimes highly intelligent people who have simply wasted their talents, putting all of their energy into the business of supplying their addiction with their drug of choice. A drug addict can do almost anything they put their minds to, given the fact that they have learned how to supply their $400 a day drug habit while being unemployed and homeless. Oftentimes a drug addict can function with a job and still manage to get their kids up for school and get their homework done at night all the while continuing on with their drug addiction at night or while the kids are at school. Granted, this type of lifestyle never, ever lasts for very long as the disease continues to demand more and more. Soon their disease overwhelms their commitments to children, spouse and job and they are homeless and destitute. The presence of the disease does not mean a lower intelligence or lack of personal talents, dreams and ambitions.

One of the ways to address the drug problem in your community is to change how alcoholics and drug addicts are perceived. Amazingly, many non-addicts see all addicts as lazy, self-centered, untalented loafers. Yet it is important to realize that they have a disease, the disease of addiction. It does not mean that they are untalented and unintelligent. It means that they need help, not disdain.

I am not saying all drug addicts are misunderstood geniuses and should be seen as potential mini-Stephen Hawkings or Eleanor Roosevelts or Thomas Mertons. What I am saying is this: your drug community has hidden within it natural born leaders who are wasting their lives in the depths of their disease...and many of them are sitting in your local, county jail.

Growing Pains and Joys

I would say that the best teacher in life is experience itself. There was no graduate program I could visit that would have taught me more than being in the Knox County Jail with the inmates themselves. I had to know the inmates and the jail milieu in order to understand it...and I learned the hard way. These are some of the lessons I learned:

- **Arrested Development**; if one takes into consideration that the average age of drug onset is 13 (which means an amazingly large amount of those in the LAM Program started using drugs when they were 8 and 9 years old) then the issue of 'arrested development' comes into play. This means that their maturation level (emotional maturation) ceased at the age they began using drugs and/or alcohol. So if you have a 40 year old who began using drugs at age 14 then in many areas of their life they will act like a 14 year old. It is quite difficult to work with a person (especially in a group setting in a jail, of all places) when they begin acting like a child and you don't understand why. You have to understand that a huge part of recovering from addiction is this process of 'catching up to the age you really are.' This is why the 12 Steps are so vital because they 'peel off the layers' and take the person back to those gaps in maturity. Through the 4th and 5th steps as well as the 6th and 7th steps you take an inventory of your life and your actions and confess those to another person as well as begin making a list of your character defects and confess those to another person. This is tough but you have to go back into your past and find out what you missed out on and begin the process of maturing through these stages in your thirties and forties.

- **Master Manipulators**; Being a minister who grew up in a very sheltered parsonage milieu I had to learn the truth the hard way: many of the people I worked with in the jail don't mean a word they say. I mean that, literally. Generally speaking, it is impossible to spot these master manipulators but they are there (although few and far between, thank goodness) and you must be on-guard. I also have to admit that I have been fooled by the best of them. This manipulation and intimidation has led to the program being jeopardized as well as my safety being compromised. You must prepare yourself for this level of lying and manipulating and bullying from another person you are trying to help, trying to minister to in the name of the God of the Universe. Yet they are there and they are people who have little to no conscience about this lying and manipulating. As a minister you must understand that any facility that incarcerates felons is a dangerous place. You must understand that you need to be very discerning regarding your ministry and you must trust and cooperate with the professional jail staff. The law enforcement personnel and the relationships I have had with them have been some of the best experiences of my LAM ministry. I have a great deal of respect for law enforcement because I have seen what they have to put up with day in and day out. For sure they see the world differently than I do yet they are trying to maintain order in a world that is based on anarchy. This is a tough place to work year after year! You must respect the law enforcement personnel first and foremost and learn from them. You must be wise which means this: learn how to keep you idealism yet lose the naïve attitude of your youth. This isn't a game anymore. This isn't a little mission trip to an Arizona Indian Reservation. This is real stuff. As a minister in this setting you must utilize St. Paul's armor of God which he mentioned prominently in Ephesians 6:10-18. The heart of that passage is the fact that the issue of salvation is contained in the 'helmet.' You must have your 'head about you' at all times. This means that you should never think that everything that everyone tells you is the truth, because it isn't. People lie and will try and manipulate you because you are a minister. Your job is to figure out a way to discern the truth, as best you can.

- **Rip Van Winkles**; I created a new class several years ago called 'current events.' As you have guessed it is about current events in today's society. I would bring in one magazine and one magazine only: "The Week." I would say that it is the only magazine you need if you want to catch up on and be informed about what is going on in today's confusing landscape of politics, entertainment, climate change, science, real estate and anything else that is important. I read directly from this magazine which gives the liberal, conservative and moderate viewpoints from journalists from around the world. It is truly a wonderful resource for our ministry and one which I would recommend highly to anyone interested in this sort of angle. I taught this class for both the men's and women's group for one reason: to get them up to speed with the world around them. It is far easier (and therefore more dangerous) to be 'institutionalized' as an inmate in today's world because the world is changing so very fast. The world around us is changing so quickly (especially in technology) that an inmate must be made aware of how very fast it really is changing. An inmate being released to a world of changing technology, politics, economics, climate change and personal health issues (just to name a few) can easily be inundated and intimidated by all of this rapid change. If they are not prepared for (or at least aware of) this plethora of change in our world today then they are more susceptible to relapsing. As Tania Willis has said often, the existence of a typical drug addict is so myopic and selfish. They have lived their life in such isolation and selfishness that many times it is this backwardness and ignorance of the world which causes a relapse, then the cycle of isolation and destruction continues for them as well as their family. A true ministry must be well-rounded in its approach to recovery.

- **Game Face**; I had to realize that since I was not a recovering addict that I had to come full force with the only weapon I had: my sincerity. I had to be totally sincere with them at all times. This meant that I gave it everything I had all of the time. What did this look like? It meant that I was willing to cuss and yell at them and tell them to their face that I wasn't afraid of them. I yelled and screamed in order to do one thing: get their attention. One doesn't begin to recover and heal unless your condition worsens to the point of deflation. Sometimes a person needs to be told to their face, "Hey, if you haven't noticed it yet, you are locked up in a county jail wearing pajamas 24/7 and your kids are where? And you lost your job? And your wife is cheating on you with whom, your best "friend?" And...and...this is all because you can't stop shooting meth or snorting pills or drinking yourself to sleep every night. What has happened to your life?!" I learned how to come at my job like: 'this guy's killing himself and I need to wake him up RIGHT NOW!' I enjoyed saying to participants "It's pretty sad when I am more passionate about your life than you are!" or "You talk about loving your kids so much but you are really just a liar!" or "Don't you ever get tired of living a life where no one believes a word you say?" or "Why would you think you have been a good Dad? It sounds as though you have been selfish and abusive to your children." I have said these things and many other harsh things to people at rock bottom. Why did I say 'enjoy'?...because when I say harsh and honest things to addicts I am not saying them to them, I am saying them to the disease. Delbert Boone told me a great litmus test for drug rehabilitation work: "Is the disease talking or their recovery talking?" When I have my 'game face' on it is not directed toward that person, it is directed right at the disease itself. Why so harsh? Because this disease is trying to do two things: **1) isolate that person and 2) destroy that person.** This is the calling card of evil itself. I can't speak from a position of recovery because I am not in recovery myself. Therefore the only angle I have is this theological position which speaks directly to the issue of salvation and eternal life. I don't know about you but I think salvation and eternal life are pretty important to a Christian (at least they should be).

- **Mr. Worley**: One of the greatest teachers I ever had was an old English teacher named Mr. Worley. He taught Senior English at Columbus East High School in Columbus, Indiana (graduated in 1986). He had an amazing, Socratic approach to teaching, one which has made a deep impression on me. One of the aspects I employed in my LAM ministry in his honor is his habit of dressing in the same clothes every school day. He had several outfits of the same pants, shirt and (Mr. Roger's cardigan) sweater which he wore every day to class. One day one of my classmates asked him why he did this and he answered, "So that I am consistent to my students in every way." In this tradition I wore the same wool sports jacket (even in the hot summers) every day to the jail (along with a plethora of 70's and 80's neck ties I have purchased for .26 cents apiece from St. Vincent de Paul's thrift shop in Vincennes) until that jacket is torn and unwearable. Many, many drug addicts have had no mature and sober adult in their life who was consistently supportive of them. They have no idea what this looks. I want to be the same person every day for them, every day.

- **Maslow's Self-Actualization**: One of the best pieces of curriculum LAM ever purchased (with United Way funding, by the way) was a short lecture on dvd by the late Delbert Boone called "Maslow's Hierarchy of Needs." In it he breaks down the entire idea of chemical addiction by applying Maslow's Hierarchy of Needs. In the original hierarchy of needs (published in 1943) Maslow posits that human behavior is ruled by their needs which are roughly divided into:

1) Biological and Physiological needs- air, food, drink, shelter

189

2) Safety needs- protection from elements, security, order, law, freedom from fear
3) Love and belongingness needs- friendship, intimacy, affection and love
4) Esteem needs- achievement, mastery, independence, status, dominance, self-respect, prestige, and respect from others
5) Self-actualization needs- realizing personal potential, self-fulfillment, seeking personal growth and peak experiences [1]

This has been a tremendous help for me to get a grasp of the idea of addiction and its nature. I think when you can get a grasp of an idea you begin to work toward understanding on a much better level. Maslow's genius was to be able to articulate human behavior in such a way as to open doors to others worlds. In this case the world of addiction. In short, humans have needs which have to be met in order to live a happy and meaningful life. When these basic needs are NOT met then problem begin to occur. Yet, chemical dependency is such a horrible reality in so many people's lives because it is so powerful that these basic human needs are ignored, discarded and forgotten. The drug or the drink takes the place of personal growth, relationship with god, with your spouse, with your friends. The drug takes the place of caring about your own hygiene, your own personal safety, your own stability and your own home. The drug takes the place of caring about your job and finally the drug takes the place of caring about basic shelter, food, water and sleep. Oftentimes (not always) it is only when a person hits this last stage of NOT caring about their biological needs will a person change. This is Maslow's version of hitting rock bottom (Dr. Karl Jung's 'deflation'). I have seen this over and over again with drug addicts and alcoholics. This is why any drug rehab program needs to address the issue of the basic needs before any real follow-up can take place. This is why we needed the transition housing before we could progress as a ministry. We needed to address these basics needs first before we could move on to the fun stuff: self-actualization.

- **Spiritual Development:** I remember the gradual realization which came over my senses in 2007 and 2008 as I began to look at our county jail (any place of incarceration for that matter) was really a monastery in disguise. It is a place, a holy space for real, intense and meaningful spiritual development to take place. Why? Because it (a jail or prison) is primarily a place of suffering and substantial and lasting growth takes place primarily in the midst of intense human deprivation and suffering. The moment someone gets comfortable in a jail is when they begin to become institutionalized. One should never, ever become comfortable in a jail. It should be the most miserable experience of their life. If it isn't, then something is very, very wrong with their life and they have a troubled existence. My mentor from seminary Dr. Charles Ashanin said to me once, "When you suffer, know that God has begun to answer your prayers." I have been blessed to minister to people in profound suffering. I appreciate Sheriff Luce and Sheriff Morris for allowing me to spend the heart of my professional ministry saying "wake up" to those people who are experiencing profound suffering in our county jail. The Knox County Jail was my parish, my church, my mission field. It should be yours too! Your local jail is the center of suffering in your community and you need to ask your faith community this question (if you aren't already ministering to that facility): why aren't we in the jail providing comfort and hope and love to those most in need? How could we miss this golden opportunity to do fantastic, front-line ministry? Why do we spend so much time in the 'church' worrying about overseas or national mission projects where we can spend tremendous amounts of money and energy going to a place, work on some tangible projects, feel good about ourselves then fly home and return to the comfort of our own cushy life when all the while the real mission field is our county jail? Why? I believe a great deal of church activity is just about making ourselves feel good and holy. I would much rather be in the 'trenches' fighting for those who have no voice. The bottom line is this: the combination of incarceration and addictions makes a drug rehab ministry in a jail-setting an ideal place to find amazingly exciting ministry. Very exciting, indeed.

- **Self-Sabotaging:** One of the most tragic traits which addicts have is that of self-sabotaging. I have seen so many men and women come so very far in their recovery with a job and a new house and the custody of their children and then right as they are about to achieve the next step on this arduous journey they intentionally relapse or quit or cheat on their spouse or miss a probation appointment or something to completely derail their progress. Then I would meet them back in another pod of the jail after their re-arrest, we would go to the classroom and begin over again, trying to learn from this and discover why they intentionally sabotaged their success. (more about this later)

Some of the Lessons from the Housing Program

The history of the LAM Houses begins with the opening of the women's house on May 31st, 2013 and the men's house soon after on October 9, 2013. We survived many ups and downs but none as trying and difficult as the devastating house fire at the Men's House on March 16, 2016 which completely destroyed our century old two-story transition home (owned by Jarod Chattin). None of the six men were injured (even Bill Wilson the house cat survived and continues to live with me and my family to this day). That night I was awakened by the house manager at 2:30 a.m. telling me the house was on fire. I rushed the six blocks to the house, noticing the plumes of smoke even in the nighttime sky above Vincennes. The cause was a gas leak but for the next few days I scrambled to find housing for the six men. Thankfully Scott Shipman and the local disaster-relief ministry called Helping His Hands opened one of their shelters and some of the six were housed until we found a new home. By the time we did find a new home only 2 of the 6 remained to start over.

Within three weeks we had found a new location and were back offering transitional housing within a month. Not very long grant you, but long enough to know a little bit more than we knew three years prior and long enough to understand even less (first comes knowing something, then comes the understanding). The anonymous person who told me the housing project would be frustrating was right. It has been very frustrating and it is risky. There are many, many things that can go wrong when you operate a transition house. But those are the risks of ministry, period. There is a huge risk of living a life in relationship with others. Yet it is the risk we are called to make as human beings, the risk of living in relationship with others. It is (absolutely) the task we are given as Christians living in the world. When I live in relationship with others I risk being disappointed and hurt and looking weak and powerless. In the work that I have done with LAM, I have met many people who have been critical of our work and ministry. This criticism comes from a few generalized groups of folks:

1) Powerlessness; many, many people in our society CAN'T appear to be weak. Christianity is seen in some Nietzschian sort of way as the religion of the meek and weak, reserved for those who are too shy and fearful to truly practice. Christianity is waning in America, even with the advent of a frightened and desperate and loud conservative right. Christianity is waning because it has lost its therapeutic power to heal, no longer a voice of hope and grace and love but providing only a voice of fear and control and political domination, all couched in talk of the end-times and judgement and the Kingdom of God. Christianity needs to rediscover its inward powers with its inherited ability to truly provide a way to clean the inside of the cup. The answers are all there, all you have to do is be at a place where you are able to listen and hear.

2) Control-freaks; many, many (secretly) fearful folks are control-freaks. They are afraid of getting hurt through their vulnerability. What are they vulnerable to? They are vulnerable to the chaos of living in relationship with others. When you have a relationship with an addict you are very, very vulnerable. There is NO way to be certain of the outcome when you work with an addict. You can do anything and everything to help that addict secure a new life with job, housing, church, etc. Christianity is in such dire condition today (at least in the U.S.) because it imitates our sick society. You see this in the modern worship/entertainment style so evident in many of the mega-churches and the small-scale

churches trying to attract new members. You also see it in our theology which has acquired a dangerous business-model to it: we only see value in ministry if we can define it as 'successful.' This success is defined as abstinence from drugs, a full-time job and reunification with their family, etc. Given, this definition of success IS the goal of LAM. However, ministry cannot be seen as a success only if these expected outcomes are met. I have seen several successes from addicts who 'on paper' are failures; i.e. have relapsed and returned to jail or were kicked out of our LAM House. I have learned that you must be willing (as a ministry) to be a 'seed planter.' In other words you must be willing to work with a person for months and even years and NOT see the results, not witness the 'product.' Many times a ministry or a minister or a layperson gets an ego trip out of our 'successes.' We like these successes because it makes us look holy and smart and trail-blazing. Ministry can be very selfish if one doesn't watch out.

To live in relationship with people is indeed very risky. It causes you to look small and powerless. It makes you feel helpless and used, manipulated. Yes. It does. Here are some of the things I have learned the most from watching people relapse and recover, relapse and recover, relapse (if you are reading this and you're a recovering addict and/or alcoholic please know that I say this with the utmost respect, since I am not in recovery. These observations are just from my experience directing the LAM ministry and being in relationship with many people who are in recovery);

- **Respect for the disease;** the most humbling aspect of our ministry has come from our transition program.

To watch people in recovery has been agonizing. It causes you to look at the disease of addiction with new eyes and realize that it indeed has a power to isolate and destroy like no other.

- **Children;** if there is one common thread which runs through almost all of the success stories within the LAM ministry it is: children. Children are a tremendous motivator for many, many addicts as they work through all of the ups and downs of recovery (particularly in the first few months and years). The vast majority of drug addicts and alcoholics had a very, very poor childhood, characterized by physical and psychological abuse, abandonment or negligence. They swore up and down on their grandmother's Bible that they would never, ever do that to their children, yet here they are, watching their own transformation into their mother or father, stepfather or foster mom, etc. They have ended up in jail and have or are about to lose custody of their child or children. The most successful men and women in our program have utilized the Lam House as a beginning point with DCFS and the county courts to begin building a case that they are willing and able to get custody of their children again and they are serious THIS time in their recovery. We have seen quite a bit of success at the women's house as it is used as a place where the children can come for short visits, then overnights, then weekends and holidays and eventually a place of their own(sometimes the first stable home/apartment they have ever had as a clean and sober family). Carly C. says, "the LAM House offered me a safe place with structure to get on my feet….It has forced me to grow in my communication [skills as well as] being able to save money, get a car and get my license back [as well as] have a safe place for my children to come and stay the night. We are like a family..."

- **Humility/Pride;** one of the greatest obstacles a recovering addict has to face is within himself or herself. You must be willing to ask for help and say to your family, your kids but mostly to your-self: I can't do this alone. This is of particular importance for the men in recovery. The vast majority of men in recovery have this false-sense of machismo which prevents them from asking for help. They feel that they can do it on their own and they don't need any help at all.

- **Old Friends;** if you aren't willing to leave your old 'friends' and work on a new community of recovering addicts then you won't stay clean very long. This is a huge problem for men and women. This issue goes hand-in-hand with the issue of loyalty which we spoke of earlier. Many addicts find sobriety but have to choose between their old lifestyle and friends and their new sober life on the other hand. Many of their old friends feel betrayed by this new life and accuse the person in recovery of being aloof and arrogant. They will say "Oh you found Jesus!" or "he's in the LAM program now, he don't have time for us anymore." There is the accusation that they have betrayed their upbringing and their family. The addict in recovery needs to understand that if he or she is going to stay clean and sober oftentimes this means that (at least) for a while they must choose their new sober life or and above their family and friends who are still in active addiction.

- **Self-Sabotaging;** don't be afraid to succeed!!! I have seen so many, many people who do so well for a period of time and get right up to the edge of success with a job or with their marriage or with their children and then completely fall-off and relapse. They throw all of the progress into the garbage can and end-up back in jail looking at more felony charges and more isolation from their friends and family and children. Why? There are as many answers to this as there are addicts. A few insights I have at least touch on the issues: 1) comfortability; he or she doesn't know what to do with success. They KNOW how to do drug addiction and the business of making a living as a rebel, bootlegging, meth-cook. 2) money; why would they want to start over and work a job at McDonalds AND Wendys when they can make money selling dope? 3) great expectations; he or she returns to the life they know and then there aren't any expectations placed upon them. No pressure. 4) loyalty; it is much easier to rely on established family and friends instead of waiting to form new bonds and relationships. 5) no work ethic; this issue goes for many sober people as well, but very few members of our human race want to put the work into true achievement. You must have the work-ethic in order to achieve anything of worth. If you cannot get this idea engrained in your head, then you won't make it. Too many of us take the path of least resistance. Nothing worthwhile is obtained for free (ask a jack-pot lottery winner). 6) personal debt; by the time you have an addict (who has been in addiction since they were in their mid-teens) reach their mid-thirties or forties they have gathered-up a substantial amount of monetary debt. This comes from multiple trips to the emergency room and hospital stays in intensive care from episodes of overdosing, college debt from a few attempts at starting over and getting a degree, child-support, massive credit card debt and attorney and court/probation fees, etc. etc. The build-up of debt is so massive, embarrassing and complicated that many addicts in recovery just avoid the subject, keep spending themselves deeper into debt or begin using again to hide from the chaos. It is much, much easier to get high than it is to face all of these stressors. It is much easier to hide away on the dope couch than it is to grow up and face reality as a son, a mother, a father, a daughter, a tax-paying citizen like the rest of us.

- **Relationships;** I can say this without equivocation: the single biggest contributor to an addict or alcoholics relapse is stress from romantic relationships. Period. In the 12 Step Program they even have a name for it: '13th Stepping.' There are only 12 Steps, (to point out the obvious) so the 13th step is when you go to a 12 step meeting and 'hook up' with someone and begin ignoring the work you need to be doing on your-self. There is a standard rule in the 12 Step Program that you don't need to have ANY kind of relationship with anyone for the first year of sobriety. In fact the vast, vast majority of those who have failed at the LAM House and been removed or who removed themselves have done so because of a relationship problem. It wasn't even drug-use that got them into trouble. It was getting into a relationship too quickly. The issue of 'arrested development' is key here: when you take a 25 year old who has been using for 10 years and they suddenly decide to get clean and sober, they are on the emotional level of a 15 year old. Until they get some time and some good drug rehabilitation programming under their belt and they mature, then they are essentially unable to truly be in a healthy relationship with someone else. Very few addicts in recovery are able to handle any type of romantic relationship for the first year of recovery. Suggestion: get a house plant first and try and keep it alive for the first year.

Prodigal Sons and Daughters

I am assuming that you and your community would like to have stories like these, giving your community hope that it can recover from the war on drugs. As I have stated before, LAM and our story is not a boastful one. I am not saying that we have THE answer to all your problems regarding a crisis of addiction in your community. What I am saying is our story is one which demonstrates what a caring community can do when it becomes united. You will need:

- Creativity (think outside the box)
- Compromise (the ability to choose your battles wisely)
- Compassion (the power to gain energy by showing grace)

in order to patiently organize your community toward this goal. But it can be done. You have to ask your community if you are willing to say: this MUST be done.

If you are going to go for it, you must be aware of several things before becoming involved in a drug rehabilitation ministry in your local jai and/or your local community. It is important to not have high expectations or better yet, don't have any expectations at all. There is saying in AA/NA: "expectations are premeditated resentments." This is wise advice indeed because believe me, you will be disappointed.

The reason the issue of expectations is so vital to what we are doing is because of the reality of relapses. Relapses are a natural and tragic part of recovery. I have seen some extremely well-meaning, loving Christian members of our Knox County community get excited about working with participants in our program, until...there is a relapse on drugs and/or alcohol followed by an arrest and incarceration. This well-meaning volunteer gets very disillusioned, and I can understand why. But what oftentimes happens next is sad and tragic too: that well-meaning and good-hearted LAM volunteer just stops any contact with the LAM participant and the LAM recovery community. The volunteer feels betrayed by the LAM participant and sometimes (not always) feels betrayed by our program and blames our program. If you are going to truly be invested in ministry with the population you must toughen up. You must toughen up and realize that sadly enough relapses are a part of recovery. It is a difficult proposition indeed to be in relationship with others, especially those with addictions. Relationships are difficult enough when dealing with people, but if there is one thing that is valued above others when it comes to dealing with recovering addicts, it is loyalty: staying loyal to an addict when they are 'down and out' after a relapse is like storing up gold. It is incredibly valuable! You must learn how to see a person through a crisis and not be manipulated and 'taken for a ride.' This is an amazingly fine line yet it is absolutely mandatory.

You and your ministry need to be the voice in your community for those who don't have a voice. You need to go into the jail and say to the people living at rock bottom: "I believe in you!" And when you say this you are looking straight into their eyes...why? Because...YOU MEAN IT! You believe in that person! The truth is, almost all of the people who tell me they are done with drinking and drugging are sincere at that moment. Why? Because they are desperate and they are experiencing 'fox-hole religion' or 'jail-house Jesus.' Jail-house Jesus is fine with me. It doesn't matter to me that most people turn their backs on all of their jail-houses promises made to God, their girlfriends, their moms and their children. It is true, many of these addicts will relapse EVEN THOUGH they truly believe they are finished with their drug use.

You and your ministry need to be ready to watch many of your participants relapse. You can't disconnect your ministry with everyone who relapses. You must discern who you are going to assist in your ministry. Some will be good decisions. Some will be bad decisions. When they are 'bad' and they relapse and return to jail in a blue paper jump suit, it is tough. This is tough because it makes you look unprofessional, weak and clueless. But you must be willing to 'see an addict through.' This takes prayer and discernment on your part. It means you must know who to continue to work with even as they relapse. It means you must be willing to cut-ties with those who you believe are not sincere. Many times an addict has several rock-bottom events in their life as an addict. The key is: you need a good, solid and mature group of recovering addicts to help you discern who is sincere and who is not. People can fool me all day...I am a minister who is NOT in recovery from addiction. But it is nearly impossible for an addict to fool other addicts. They know the twists and turns of logic, the lies and manipulations of loved ones, the theft of property and trust. ***The addict helping another addict is the key.*** This is what LAM has done: we created a new community of recovering addicts...and this is what you must do to combat the drug problem in your community. But be warned: the creation of a new community of recovering addicts is no simple and easy task. It takes patience and prayer, and lots of both.

I believe in you...but you are a horrible criminal.

There are so many young men and women who are drug addicts, alcoholics and wannabe thugs and thugettes who are horrible criminals. They are terrible at thieving and robbing and stealing and continue to be rearrested time and time again. The reason? Simply put: they aren't criminals, they are drug addicts. The 12 Steps and God help you figure out WHY you are a drug addict. It is this discovery as to WHY that is key. In order to discover this WHY you must be given time and space. This is why the jail program is so vital. It offers people who are in physical, psychological and spiritual pain (and in turn are harming their community) an opportunity to discover who they are.

Who does that anymore? Self-discovery? In discovering who you really are (as opposed to all the masks we wear on any given day) we find that we re-discover who God is in our life. The word 'religion' literally means 'to re-link.' When I see a drug addict sitting in county-issued pajamas waiting for their food tray (as the high-light of their day) I don't see a worthless, dead-beat dad who can't get their life together long enough to hold down a job and take care of their kids. I see a prodigal son! I see a prodigal son who has hit rock bottom. I see a prodigal son who has just begun to think about returning home to his father's farm where even the servants are well-fed and clothed and care for, yet here he is competing with the pigs for a scrap of food. I see the prodigal son incarnate, sitting in our county jail just waiting for someone to tell him it is alright to go home. It is alright to go home.

It's alright for your community to heal as well. The following section is designed to give your community guidance if it is at a place where it can begin the healing process from a battle with addictions. It is included here as a check-list and discussion starter for small group(s). It all begins and ends with a community coming together and healing together.

Opening questions for your community regarding starting a program

Community Leadership

- Who is the County Sheriff/chief law enforcement officer? Would he be willing to talk meet with local leaders of our faith community regarding a jail program?
- Who are the local political leaders? Would they be willing to talk with local leaders of our faith community regarding a drug rehab program in our community?
- Who are your leaders of your law enforcement community?
- Who are the business leaders in our community?

Christian Community?

- Are we a 'just' and loving Christian meritocracy where hard work and dedication can earn you a good living and a future for your family?
- Are we a community based on peace and love and harmony?
- Do we truly reach out and offer a helping hand to those in need?

- Can a community be a true community (Christian or not) and continue to ignore the plight of the lowest on the socio-economic ladder?
- Can a community be a 'Christian community' while allowing unabated suffering continue in their county jail?
- What type of service organizations and ministries do you have in your community? What do they do? (be specific regarding each population served)
- How many churches does our community have? Do we have any 'ministerial association' which organizes community worship and Christian activities? If so, when and where does it meet?
- Make a list the Christian leaders (ordained or not) in our community (name, church and role in each church)
- Is our faith community mature enough to start an ecumenical organization which is willing to put aside political and doctrinal differences in order to reach a common goal?

How Big Is Our Drug Problem?

- Do we have a drug problem in our community?
- On a scale of 1-10 ('1' being no pain at all and '10' being overwhelming pain) what is the level of pain our community is experiencing because of our drug problem?
- What kind of chemical addiction problem does our community have? (be specific)
- Are children suffering in our community? (do you even know, other than rumor?)

- What do your local CHINS (or the equivalent) stats report?
- What types of services are established in our community which specifically minister to children and youth?
- How could you best minister to your local children?
- Is there is jail ministry in our community? If so, what is it, what do they do and how long have they been doing it?
- What kind of women's jail ministry does our community provide? Who does it and what does it do?
- Who in our faith-community feels called to jail ministry? How dedicated are they?
- Are they willing to speak with you and the leaders of the church community about the possibility of a jail ministry?
- Do you know anyone who is willing to do research for start-up grants as well as to write grants to begin your project?

I don't care if you are a minister or a social work student, your community has a drug problem, period. My question to you is this: what are you doing about this? This drug problem you have in your community is way, way bigger than you think, whether you like it or not. It is way bigger than you can handle by yourself or any one organization, church or county hospital can handle alone. You need to collaborate, you need partners and you all need to be on the 'same page.' You need mobilize and direct your community in the right direction if this is going to work.

Concrete Steps Towards a Ministry

Step One

Your first step after you have determined some of your community's drug and alcohol-related issues should be to organize a meeting of your leaders in your community. You should include members or a few members from:

- Faith community:
- Law enforcement community:
- Local political leaders:
- Business community:
- Recovery community:
- Family of drug addicts:
- Concerned citizens:

This list is not exhaustive. Please add to it, but the takeaway point is this: you need the leaders of your community to meet in one room at the same time without outside distractions and ask some serious questions. This is a community problem and needs to be addressed by your community. i.e. you don't need people on any personal crusade to show everyone 'how it's done.' You need team players who are willing to sustain that energy as a team, not individuals. You need to ask yourselves these types of questions:

- What are some of our community's strengths?
- What are some of our community's weaknesses?
- What kind of history does our community have with addictions?

- What kind of addiction problems did we have 20 and 10 years ago?
- What kind of addiction problems do we have today?
- What kind of assistance does our community offer drug addicts and alcoholics?
  If so, what/who does this programming or ministry?
- Do we have any type of programming in the local jail? If not, who would volunteer to speak with the local Sheriff regarding the possibility of starting a drug rehabilitation ministry/program in his or her county jail?
  (this point it relevant only if the sheriff has not been contacted already or is not in attendance at this meeting)

Step Two

Let us assume that your local Sheriff agrees with your mission and patient and kind enough to allow you to begin work on implementing this program in his/her local jail. The next step is three-pronged:

1). Choose a few volunteers from your original group to form a board of directors. Nominate and elect officers for your board of directors to begin the formation of a not-for-profit organization. Meet and begin the process of forming a 501c3 as well as by-laws to guide your new 501c3. Find an attorney who can help lead you in this legal step in the formation of a firm foundation to your organization.

2). Choose a sub-committee to begin to investigate a specific community-model program for your jail ministry.

3). Investigate who in your community would be willing to help to begin to work on finding suitable grants to help fund your program in the jail.

Step Three

The next steps will be up to you and your community. These are merely suggestions which I humbly offer to you and your community. There is no one on Earth who can tell you what will happen next, let alone what to do. But this book has been written to help you get started with the process. This process of starting a new drug-rehabilitation program is very, very organic, with a life of its own. Each community has different traits and characteristics which will require patience and ingenuity and humility. This is a tough task to take on, make no mistake. It is a process that needs to grow in relationship to the needs of your own community. The only way to truly know the needs of your community is to get 'your hands dirty' and get to know your community from down in the trenches. The best place to get to know the needs of your community is by asking those people who are in the greatest amount of pain. This group of people is found among those suffering from addictions. You will find most of them sitting in your county jail. Now, have at it.

Part IV: Full Human Interaction

"Most profoundly, [sobriety] was a conversion from the destructively total self-centeredness to the fourth aspect of the core idea: constructive, creative, and *fully human interaction* with others."

-Ernest Kurtz, "Not-God" (pg 34)

Indeed Professor Kurtz was correct when he observed that this conversion from a self-centered existence to a "constructive, creative and fully human interaction with others" is what a person living in sobriety looks like...this is it. I again return to William Heuby for some insights into this fourth aspect of the core idea which is at the foundation of A.A. During my last couple of years as the Director of LAM, William taught a Narcotics Anonymous class at the jail. Every Monday afternoon after he got off work at Vincennes University as an electrician he would meet me at the jail. He would walk in as a free man and walk out the same: free. We would go by the jail kitchen, talk to some of the trustees for a bit and grab a tray of that evening's supper for William to have and we would sit and talk while the LAM participants would finish their supper and prepare for class. It was always noted the irony of him coming into to do a class and eating a jail food again.

His NA class was essentially a re-entry/spirituality class which highlighted the things which worked for him in his recovery. I would sit in the back of the little classroom and jot down notes in my tiny journal I always kept in the breast pocket of my tweed jacket. On May 15, 2017 he was in particular form as he spoke of the long road which got him there;

> *I never had a friend all the way through elementary, high school and into adulthood. I didn't know what that looked like: a friend! A friend to tell all my secrets to? [expletive and laughter] When I was in the LAM Program I experienced something other than me, I call that God and what I experienced was beautiful...something amazing. The 12 Steps are designed to lead you into God-consciousness...so this is how I did it: I learned how to meditate, I did the entire steps multiple times with different sponsors and I began working within a group and I began to feed off of the energy that a group can generate. Amazing really...amazing. I mean come on guys! The whole goal of the LAM Program is to change your future and your children's future and by doing so you change the world and the life around you.*

There is really no better way to express this core idea of full human interaction than William did on that May afternoon in the Knox County Jail. There is this movement within the human being which begins with the hopelessness of the human condition, moving into a depression-like state of deflation then rising up out of this state into a building up of the energy which we call conversion. This conversion is only called conversion because it produces a different state within a fallen human being and the natural reaction of this person experiencing conversion is one thing: full human interaction. In other words, the way you can tell that a person is in recovery from an addiction is if they begin to interact with the world around them through their family, their children, their work, their church, their community, their environment and their world. They must be acting upon this conversion for it to be conversion in the first place. There must be inward action but there must also be outward reaction. There must be fruit on the tree for it to be called a fruit tree, right?

The beginning of a new community

On Halloween night of 2007 I accompanied Penny Patton and Morgan Moss around the 7 male pods (the jail has 7 male pods and 1 female pod) and interviewed any volunteer inmates for this new program which Sheriff Luce was starting: the LAM Program. These men were asked a simple question by Morgan and Penny: "Are you sick and tired of being sick and tired?"

That night we collected over 40 applications and afterward Morgan and Penny sat down in my little cubicle and sorted through them, writing 'ringer' on a dozen of them. The next morning we were accompanied by Sheriff Steve Luce and jail commander John Vendes as we gathered up the first dozen male members of the LAM Program into B pod. These were the men who were chosen because of their high level of emotional and (some of them) physical pain they had expressed during their interview...some of them were 'faking it 'til they made it' but others were genuinely ready to move ahead with their recovery, venturing into new territory with the rest of us.

Some of these men were from nearby Vanderburgh County an hour's drive to the south, so I have lost touch with them, but several in that first group are still around Vincennes. I see them from time to time...you know, around town or walking down the hallway at the Knox County Jail wearing the familiar black and white jail-issued pajamas. I remember seeing that sly look on their face that said, "what's up, Pete?" I would shake my head and offer a hand out and ask them if they want back in the program...most of them say 'not this time' or 'yea maybe, if you can come to court with me?'

Beginning in earnest in February of 2008 but in earnest by April of 2009 (when I took over the day-to-day running of the jail program from Carrie Williams) we have had a 6 week certificate ceremony to mark the end of a set of classes as well as an opportunity to invite 5-10 guests in to the jail to witness what is going on with the LAM Program. I was meticulous in taking a picture of each group, recording their names and specific certificate earned on a program (the women's program has done this since it began in May of 2010). It was amazing to look at the pictures of these men and women and see the hope in their eyes, this hope that this is going to be the end of it, the end of this nightmare of addiction which has scrambled their brain and separated them from their children and their wives and mothers and grandmothers and cousins and jobs and community.

The hope on their faces said it all, even knowing that that hope may or may not have been genuine, disguising the deep reservation that they weren't really done with using, weren't done with the fun of being an outlaw, were just using LAM for a quick certificate for court or whatever. This hope has to drive a community, driving them to express the sighs and groans as they are being inundated by the rising seas of addiction. This problem is so systemic that it is absolutely imperative that this point is reiterated here in the final section of this memoir.

It takes the efforts of an *entire* community to begin to find relief from the impact of addiction

These efforts need to begin in the local jail, offering hope to the hopeless so that seeds of recovery are planted within the scarred minds and bent and bruised souls of these addicts we call inmates. These efforts have to begin somewhere and sometime with some program. Otherwise your community will continue to be at the mercy of the economics of the opiate game in America as well as the sinister preying of other entities and nations upon our citizens who inject our nation with an endless supply of synthetic drugs such as bath salt and K2. If you do not come together as a community and fight this war on drugs (which is raging all around you) then you will continue to be subject to not only the forces of the present which are preying upon us, but you will also be subject to all of the ghosts of the past, hiding in the history of our country's fascination with war and the inevitable association with the drugs of choice which follow in the direct footsteps of the soldiers on the ground and in the air and in the seas. Your community is subject to outside forces until it seizes control of these 'gates' and begins to prevent these influences from having such easy access to the poor, the destitute, the disabled and the downtrodden. You must regain control of your community!!

If drugs are an existential attempt at escaping the pain and boredom of human existence, then a good recovery program is an aggressive attempt at RECONNECTING a human life with the humanity they have been aggressively disconnecting themselves from their entire life...

As we have seen in Professor Kamienski's work, the impact of drugs and warfare have impacted those societies at war with the result being a *disconnection with the civilized world.* When you look at the etymology of the word 'religion' it quite literally means to 're-link.' That is what a good drug rehabilitation program does: it re-links the drug addict and alcoholic with his or her 'self, their family, their community and their God. When we do this, we call it "full human interaction" as Ernest Kurtz would say. This disconnection with the civilized world is a serious business. It seems to me that there are sinister forces at work in the communities of America. The fact that we are at continual war (no matter what administration is in the White House) is a disturbing fact. Since 2002, our country has had no time to recuperate from the last war, continually being infected by the brutality and violence. This chaos is brought right back home and shot directly into the heart of America. Our

215

communities (many of them rural and poor) have to figure out what to do with this chaos and right now, all we are doing is building bigger jails. We have to be in those jails and help those who are ready to get out of the chaos.

Untying the knots

The beauty and dynamism of the 12 Steps is that they begin with the disconnected person and slowly 'untie the knots.' In the tradition of Mr. Worley (my senior English teacher at Columbus East High School) I used to wear the same wool jacket (yes, the kind with the patches on the elbows) to the jail each day. I wore them each day until they wore themselves out (I went through six wool jackets since 2007) and I put all of my toys and paperclips and pens and small journal in my pockets of the new jacket. I also placed a bit of shoe lace in the pocket of the new jacket. It was a shoe string a young kid named Jeremy gave me once when asked for one real quick to demonstrate their life in recovery.

I began to tie the already tattered shoelace into knot after knot after knot. Some of the knots were tightly pulled one after another, while others were somewhat loose. I liked to bring this out once in a while and toss it on someone's lap and say, "here, why don't you try and untie this top knot." The knot is so tight it impossible to untie it quickly if at all. I smile and say, "this is your life now...after years of tying your life up into knot upon knot with broken relationships, hepatitis c infection, three kids by three separate women and a book-in sheet 36 pages long and two prison terms...so you might as well sit back and relax because it's gonna take a little bit to untie all of these beautiful knots you have tied for yourself."

This is how our addicts are...this is how our families are...this is how our communities are and this is how our country is...we have to slowly begin to untie these knots. The way a community does this is to be fully involved in the addict's life. This full human interaction begins in the jail and moves out into the community.

Kathy

You want to talk about a life tied up in knots?! Let me tell you about a LAM participant whose life was complicated at an early age through absolutely no fault of her own and she has spent the rest of it trying to untie the knots. Her story is the story of hundreds of thousands of women in this country who struggle with recuperating from sexual abuse at a young age yet who end-up in jail and prison. It is the pinnacle of injustice that such wonderful people have their life stolen from them by perverts and pigs and yet have no one there to help them recover their lost childhood. Their appearance in the county jails of this country is one of the saddest sagas of our time. Here is just one story;

`I have already spoken of her before: Kathy Borden. She (along with Steve Seale) was one of the leaders of the drug community in Knox County, one who was quite well-known at the jail by both inmates and staff and in the recovery community. In other words, she was pretty notorious for her thuggishness in and out of the jail. If 'Kat' ('Kat' was her street persona, lol) was involved you knew she was in control. She had a proclivity for getting her way and being very charming while doing it, yet she could be brutal. I had heard of her, in particular due to her ex-husband Jon being in the very first men's group back in November 2007, but I had never met her. It wasn't until Tania began working with me and we began to recruit in the women's pod. I remember Tania asking Sheriff Morris if we could place Kathy in the program and he just laughed. Tania and I didn't think it was so funny...why would the Sheriff be so narrow-minded?

Kathy is 5'8" ish, brown hair with the look of suburbian soccer mom. I could always picture her driving around town in her van on her way to pick up her kids but looks can be tragic. Like so many of the men and women I have dealt with, I would often look at them and see the lines drawn on their faces from years of abuse and neglect and abandonment as well as the toll of the drugs and alcohol and wonder what they would look like without this tremendous burden that was placed upon them at such an early age? I wonder how I would have dealt with this burden at the age of 4 or 5? Why was I spared this burden?

I sat down with Kathy a few months ago at a local Mexican Restaurant and I asked her permission to include her story in the story of LAM. She said yes and she began to tell me her story. During the few women's groups that I would sit in on and some of her talks at churches I had heard bits and pieces of her story, yet I had never heard it from stem to stern. The first thing she remembered was how her father was constantly abusive to her mother. She said her earliest memories are of her waking up hearing her Father abusing her mother. All the way to age 11 her mother endured this abuse, yet from age 9 to 11 Kathy herself endured a horror of her own: molestation.

During this crucial time in Kathy's life she had to survive sexual molestation by her uncle. She would see him daily at her grandmother's house, oftentimes staying overnight with him. She would 'act-out' in front of her Father in order to try and stay away from her uncle yet the abuse continued until her parents divorced when she was 11 and she and her mother moved to Florida. It was during her time in Florida that she began to drink and use ecstasy. It was also at age 11 that she discovered she was adopted. She soon met her biological mom (who lived in Virginia) and not long after this meeting she was introduced to acid. Eventually she and her adopted mother moved back to Indiana (after her adopted father died) and by the age of 21 she had become a single-mother. She met her first husband Jon and they began a relationship which replicated the abusive relationship of her adopted parents.

Eventually the stress from this abusive marriage and the drama which it brought to her eerily familiar life led her to begin using meth. Meth was the so amazing in her life: it gave her the confidence to begin to defend herself...it gave her a new persona, one who was in control of her life and anyone else's life she came in contact with...she became 'Kat' and now she was the bully, she was in control.

Yet the meth only caused more chaos, as her chaotic lifestyle and behavior began to be noticed by society and her children were taken away. She soon left Jon and hit it hard, starting to cook meth now, going deeper and deeper into this new underworld of meth in the heartland of America. She began to shoot meth to get a quicker high and her life spiraled out of control.

I remember that she and I made eye contact during this point in the interview as she paused and said, "I loved the needle more than I loved my kids."

To Kat, meth was the dependable companion she had always desired. She had never had anyone remain loyal to her. She had never had anyone to defend her. She had never had anyone who would love her unconditionally...until meth. Meth was her only dependable friend...her loyal, big brother who protected her from all the bad guys...her constant companion. It gave her the strength to survive and control her life and the men around her. Meth allowed her to be the person she always needed to be in order to survive a world where all of the grown-ups are so screwed up and narcissistic that the children are literally left to fend for themselves. Meth was there for her. Meth was there.

Full Human Interaction

One of the most wondrous aspects of the LAM Program for me was the feeling of being in the 'trenches' (excuse my militaristic imagery). I love (and I do mean the word 'love') ministry or social work when it is working with people who really want to change. The jail is the absolute perfect place for this to happen and it is the most underestimated places in America for true ministry and vital social work. When you break it all down, any type of societal evolution begins and ends with the individual person, their growth and edification and advancement. As Dr. Ashanin said, if we don't work toward a higher state of consciousness then we are nothing more than crawling creatures, we are nothing more than ants.

One of the most basic ideas which is contained within this memoir is the idea that our American county jails are packed with people who have been 'caught up' in the violence of our sick and dying civilization. In their attempt to survive and have a few moments of forgetting or brief attempts at spiritual equilibrium in their life they have engaged in obviously illegal activity and have not had the financial or social status to extricate themselves from incarceration. They have been caught up in the 'Matrix-esque' system, the broken-down and prejudicial and unjust criminal justice system of 21st Century America. At the average age of 12, they have begun using chemical substances which have altered their brain development and they are stuck in the horrific web of jail and violence and poverty and abuse on every level of their fragile life. There is an enormous amount of the 700,000 Americans who daily sit in American jails who are not criminals at all. They are abused, neglected, forgotten drug addicts still waiting for someone to ask them if they need some help. LAM and other programs like it are after **this** group of inmates who have gotten stuck in the system and cannot get out. LAM is NOT interested in the career criminal who is perennially stuck in the immaturity of their childhood who is only interested in remaining a crawling creature. We have jails for a reason. Let's keep the jails and support our law enforcement, but let's add a 12 Step-based drug rehab program in every jail. As Americans, let's learn how to separate the drug addicts from the criminals.

Shake-n-Bake Jesus and the Middle Class

As Kathy's story reveals, the issues of this extrication are numerous. I would say that it all comes down to trust. You must learn how to trust.

When you are sitting day after day listening to story after story of addicts and their histories, you begin to see patterns. It is easy for the naïve and oftentimes arrogant conservative Christian to come into the jail and just declare that all you have to do is believe that Christ died for your sins and then all will be forgiven and a new life can start. Simple, heh? I find this an embarrassing aspect of our 'modern' Christian religion in the age of Trump that the intricate nature of healing can be reduced to cute little sayings, all the while hiding racial and social prejudices. These things are obviously said by people who do not know what they are talking about, because the truth is much more difficult and the healing process much more extensive. Christianity is not a nationalistic club to be joined. It is a religion based on the healing of our psyche. This is the loving teaching of Christ which is designed to transform a life. During my LAM ministry and social work, I have seen this transformation happen. I stayed with William and Kathy and Conrad and Carly as they transformed and I saw this. I stayed with them.

This transformation...yes. But how? How? This 'how' is the missing piece of our religion which we call 'Christianity.' It commands us to love our neighbor as our "self" but we are given this awful freedom of choice and we oftentimes (as in this present, prejudicial age we live in) choose only those who look like us, sound like us and yell and scream like us. What about the 700,000 people who daily sit in American jails? What about them? They are supposed to just get released (97% of them are released to communities all over America) and walk down the street where the jail is located and pick up the pieces of their fractured life and start reaching for that middle class dream of a family, a job and taxes and mowing the lawn and picking up the kids from baseball practice? I remember catching myself in the middle of a lesson one time at the Knox County Jail and pausing, realizing to myself that what I was really saying is: 'What you need to do is join the 'American Middle Class.' Is that all this was all the time, just a social experiment? Was I really only asking people who weren't like me to become like me? Was I just a middle class white guy asking those less fortunate to be more like I am? Was I just kidding myself, no better than the arrogant, conservative Christians I see waltz into the jail and proclaim the good news of shake and bake Jesus? Was I just kidding myself?

The Difficulty of Trust

These are just a few of the problems a typical addict must face while they are sitting in a county jail;

1). One must trust. Yes. But how? How is this done when you have been let down by EVERY adult you have ever come into contact with? How? It is simply not loving (and therefore not Christian in any manner) to assume it is strictly a matter of will that someone can learn how to trust under such circumstances.

2.) One must love your 'self.' Yes. But how? How is this done when you have never had any self-respect, let alone love for yourself ever in your entire life? How? By the time you come up for air and sober up in a county jail you don't have time or space to sit and begin to examine your life and all of the self-betraying behavior you have spread throughout your life. The amount of guilt which an addict has is tremendous, this guilt many, many times is focused on abandoning their children time and time again when they promised themselves they would never abandon their children like they had been abandoned.

3.)   One must stop being co-dependent. Yes. But how? How is this done when the only manner of relationship you have ever had has been based on clinging desperately to whomever you are with at the time? This is a particular issue when it comes to women, who remain in abusive relationships trying to control them yet end up being blasted both spiritually and physically, year after year in highly dysfunctional relationships.

4.)   One must depend on a higher power. Yes. But how? How is this done when 'God' has never ever been worthy of trust? This is an acute issue when the parental abuser has been associated with a church or Christianity and the abuse and abandonment has been closely linked with 'God' himself. Where was God when I needed him?!

5.)   One must get a job? Yes. But how? How are you supposed to find a job when you have never (literally) work a day in your life and have never received an actual paycheck? Where do you start? Without assistance it is extremely difficult and depressing to be turned down for jobs over and over, end up getting a low-paying job in fast food or factory or landscaping where you are surrounded by drugs all day long by co-workers and supervisors alike.

6.)   One must get your driver's license. Yes. But how? How are you supposed to get your license back (or maybe get your license for the first time) when you have fines and costs from past violations which you cannot afford until you have work...which you cannot find...

7.)   One must get a bank account. Yes. But why? Why should you get a bank account (like a real adult) when the IRS or child-support or Vincennes University or the local hospital will come and suck it dry due to a life-time of debt which has mounted up year after year?

8.)   One must find or re-obtain a copy of their birth certificate and social security card. This means knowing where to go and what to bring and who to ask and finding a ride there and on and on...so many addicts reach this starting point toward an i.d. and just quit. It's easier to just go to CVS and buy a box and sell it for a quick $50 than to get a job...

The wake-up call

The cheesy stench of dirty feet, dirty underwear and cheap wintergreen chewing tobacco mixes in the air and it hits you: I got caught. The meth addict detoxes from meth by hibernating, sleeping the first four or five days in the jail, missing most of the meals and just getting up to urinate (if they have any liquids left in them). When they awaken they begin to see things clearly for the first time since they were on the run, up for the most part of 20 days or so (with a little cat-nap here and there). They have been hallucinating for the last several days, imagining dark figures in the bushes...the Feds hiding and waiting at Hucks when they stop to get a pack of Marlboro Lights and a Red Bull...when they're having sex with another dope whore, banging another one out as they say...over and over and they won't remember a thing...over and over...

...when a drug addict is sitting in a county jail and they sober up and realize how enormously deep their pit really is which they have fallen into over the past 10-15 years of outlawin' and thuggin'...one of the last resorts is to turn to recovery or to turn to Jesus or to try and get a job. Instead of making amends with all of these dozens and dozens of people whom they have hurt time and time again, it is much easier to just spend their time in the jail trying to get smarter at the game and just not get caught next time. So many people spend their time in the county jail as a sort of criminal college where they go and learn from the older, wiser meth cooks who can show them the 'ropes.' The vast, vast majority of an inmate's time in jail is spent waiting to get out and do it again, but smarter next time.

A jail rehab program should be all about providing the network of support for an addict to be able to have an alternative plan when they are released. This is what the full human interaction is all about: being in the trench with them. Being IN the trench but not OF the trench. Lol...Is that possible? It takes a huge amount of time and effort and patience and love to walk with people one by one as they untie these knots. Whether these knots were tied by an abusive father of foster parent or a cousin or the bus driver or maybe these knots were tied all by themselves...no matter...it takes time to turn a selfish, destructive life into a life where joy and peace and love can flow through them, oftentimes for the first time ever.

On July 17, 2017 William Heuby said this to an Narcotics Anonymous class he was teaching in the jail: "We lived in a narrow world, isolated from anyone who didn't supply us our addictive needs. Then you realize life is full of choices...then you open yourself to the possibilities of a life filled with people...the world is filled with good people."

The Houses

As we have already addressed, the most important, distinguishing characteristic about the LAM Program from other jail drug rehab programs is this: LAM has a 12 Step, faith-based program that is DIRECTLY connected to a transition housing program. The jail program feeds the housing program, seamlessly connected together. The job of the jail program is essentially one thing: to 'vet' the members for the transition houses. The ground is plowed in the jail and the seeds planted, however the transition housing is the harvest. It is that simple. Every county jail in America should have at least one of these programs for the volunteer men and women who are sick and tired of being sick and tired.

This sacred space (which we have spoken of prominently already) needs to be created both in the jail and in the transition houses so that the proper atmosphere can be there. It's very similar to planting a seed in the ground: moisture, temperature, soil condition, sunlight...it all needs to be there combining to create the right atmosphere.

The houses (in particular the men's house) are where you will see the absolute chasm which stands between the addict and a stable life of sober living. The issue of arrested development is enormous and although we have spoken of this before, it needs to be emphasized. You will have a forty year old man with spinal stenosis and a mouth full of rotten teeth yet within the first week of freedom from the jail and living in the men's house he will begin chasing the women as if he was a smooth 15 year old again, dreaming of buying a motor cycle with his first paycheck...

Rev. Steve DeFields-Gambrell and Post-Acute Withdrawal

Let me tell you about a minister and friend named Steve DeFields-Gambrell. He was the pastor of the First Christian Church (Disciples of Christ) in Vincennes and when he moved into town (as was my custom with new ministers) I introduced myself and the LAM Program. Come to find out, Steve had a tremendous amount of experience in an inpatient drug rehab program prior to entering the ministry. When I found this out, I invited Steve to come down to the jail and see the LAM Program. To make a long story short, he began to teach a relapse prevention class for our program on Thursday afternoons. Steve ended up being the best teacher we ever had, hands-down favorite of the inmates as he had a way of explaining the ins and outs, the highs and lows of a life of mature recovery. He was a progressive in his politics and theology, making him a perfect fit for me and my angle on the world, so he and I became fast friends.

Prior to his move to Indianapolis he taught a class (on April 13, 2017, 1-2 p.m.) on Post-Acute Withdrawal Syndrome or PAWS. PAWS is an essential part of understanding the true nature of a recovering addict or alcoholic and the dangers of underestimating its strength and energy during the first 3-18 months of clean-time. PAWS is a 'rewiring' of the damaged central nervous system of an addict after oftentimes years of abuse. As my notes from Steve's class attest, PAWS can impact many aspects of basic human behavior. It can impact basic thought processes with issues of craving and pre-occupation and concentration. It can impact issues of memory with euphoric recall. It can impact the emotions with issues with overreactions to good emotions as well as bad emotions, numbness, issues with sleep with bizarre dreams and nightmares. This emotional issue is why so many addicts gravitate toward very conservative religious ideas, in particular Pentecostal euphoria. It can impact issues of physical coordination, where the recovering addict can appear to act and feel as if they are drunk, yet are indeed not drunk or high. It can impact stress sensitivity with issues of over-reacting, quitting relationships and jobs and 12 Step meetings, etc...with physical symptoms of headaches, sweaty palms and back aches...

I remember the LAM participants that day recognized all of these issues and quickly asked Steve the question: what can we do about it? Steve's answer:

- self-awareness as a new lifestyle
- verbalizing your feelings, 12 Step groups, exercise, diet from sugar and caffeine
- reality checks, visualizing sobriety and goals
- meditation
- simple action plan to manage your brain, filling your mind with tangible things you can manage and change...keeping it all within reach

This is the science of recovery combined with the 12 Step program...all designed to surround the person in recovery with a new community of recovering addicts…surrounding them with the family that many of them never had but always wanted.

The Long Encounter with these Ghosts of the War

In October of 2017, Steve told me that he was leaving town and moving to Indy to be close to family. My initial reaction was selfish: I was losing my best teacher. Four weeks later I was on the phone accepting the job of Transitional Minister at Steve's old church (First Christian Church in downtown Vincennes). Ironically, Steve's departure opened up my own departure from LAM. After 10 years of hitting the trenches with these amazing soldiers in the war on drugs, I was ready to climb out of the mud and crap and take a breather. I would be returning to the place where my call to ministry began: a local church.

It has been such a long encounter with these ghosts of the war. I suppose I have done my job, just another attempt to create a new kind of family for a group of people who never had a family to begin with…maybe. Or maybe I was no different than any other lower to middle class white guy looking for a tribe to belong to…welcome to life in America where we are so pathetically needy, just whining about not belonging. What's the big deal with belonging anyway? Isn't that what got Trump elected in '16? Isn't that what fueled the alt-right after the Vietnam War? We are all just wanting to belong so badly that we would rather sell our soul to the devil than not belong to something somewhere even if, even if we turn our back on who we really are…or at least who we used to identify with back in the 80's or the 90's when everything was right with the world. A Christian? Wow, I sure sound like one, but am I really just desperate to not be alone? Is it really that simple? Am I really that transparent?

On November 17, 2017 at 7:30 a.m. in the KCAARC Board Room I told my (poorly attended) LAM Board that I was quitting. It was in that room on December 17, 2007 that I was hired full-time as the Executive Director of LAM...I remember it didn't mean much to me at the time because we were literally broke by then with no money in sight for my job or the ministry. Now, a decade later I was saying goodbye. I had enough of this war.

The Last Walk at the Jail

I remember walking down the hallway on my last day at the jail and realizing I had the luxury of walking away. What about all of these orphaned kids in the 8 pods behind me? What about the abandoned kids, the molested ones, the beaten and broken ones? What about R. A. who at 9 years old was shot-up with heroin by his big brother and who was never the same? What about G. H. who was molested by his Pentecostal Preacher at the age of 5 and was abandoned by his mother to the Old West chaos of the North End? What about H.S. whose addicted parents would just periodically abandon her at age 9 and she had to get herself and her sister fed and ready for school every day with no food in the house and no money? What about 9 year old B.B. whose stepfather molested his older sisters until he shot him to death with a shotgun? What about M. D. who at 9 years old would not steal for his father (who was also a Sheriff's Deputy) and he was kicked out of the house to go live on his own?...the stories go on and on as I walk down that hallway as I hear some random inmate yell through the door, "Trustee...G-pod...chew!" Do they ever, ever get to belong to a family? Isn't that what we all fear: not belonging to someone, to something, somewhere?

If there was anything that I would miss about LAM, it was the jail. That is the place that I always felt like I belonged. I never felt like an alien. I was always included in their terribly dysfunctional family. It was the most violent, smelliest, overpowering, claustrophobic place in Knox

County but it was haven, my sanctuary, my place of refuge and my home for a decade. I would spend more time in that place than I have any other work environment in my adult life and I loved it. It was where I belonged. These 'criminals' were not thieves and addicts to me, they were my family. They included me in their family without reservation after they realized that I was an orphan too. The labels meant nothing. We were all Americans trying to survive the chaos of a war on drugs that none of us ever signed up for. We were all just trying to survive.

Epilogue: the grand banquet hall

On February 8, 2010 LAM had its first fundraising banquet at the First Baptist Church. On February 22, 2018 LAM had its 9th Banquet (now being held at the Highland Woods Community Center). It would be my last one. Not only was it my last Banquet as the Director of the Ministry I started, it would be my last few moments as the Director. When I walked out of the doors of the Highland Woods Community Center in Vincennes, I would walk away from it all, never returning to the 'trenches' on the Knox County Jail again. I was so tired and ready for it all to be a memory.

We had a record crowd (596) and record amount of churches involved (32) and a record amount of money raised even prior to the banquet night. The banquet was the idea of one of our past LAM Board Presidents: Rev. Dan Clemens. When he moved a few years ago we lost our best board president. But he left us with this great fundraiser/rally night, which has become the biggest draw of any event in Knox County all year around.

The night of the last banquet was great weather (our fourth and fifth banquets were disasters with an ice storm one year and a tornado warning the next). There were so many LAM participants who had come to the banquet, which was not only a fundraising event but also an important social event for the LAM participants themselves to join as one family and have a night in honor of them and their families. Many of them brought their kids.

I was unusually calm that night, knowing that I had worked so hard to leave LAM in good shape financially and with a solid program in the jail for Pastor Marsha Bishop, who had been hired as the new Executive Director (Tania Willis would continue on as the Female Director).

That night's banquet would also be the last for Sheriff Mike Morris, as he was in his last year as a term-limited Sheriff of Knox County. Sheriff Morris had a 40+ year career in the Knox County Sheriff's Department. He is the real deal when it comes to cops, a guy who was all business when it came to his job, yet he knew the politics of his elected position as well as anyone. When he became Sheriff and he inherited the LAM Program from Sheriff Luce, he didn't have to keep it in his jail. Sheriff Luce didn't have to start it in the first place. But they both did it and kept it. In the early months and first couple of years of Sheriff Morris's administration I felt as though he might kick us out at any time. Yet here we were, the last night and we had made it. Our board president got up to give the Sheriff his award and the Sheriff received a standing ovation from the crowd. I grinned as I golf-clapped softly.

When it was my turn to say a few words of goodbye, I walked past the Sheriff and shook his hand and thanked him one last time. I walked up onto the stage. I recall standing up in front of my adopted community and pausing. For those few seconds I could act like I was thinking of what to say, but I wasn't...I knew what to say. I looked out and smiled, but was thinking only one thing: was I a member yet? Was I included? Was I one of them? Was this my home now? Or did I still feel like a stranger, still? Maybe I had gravitated toward these orphaned addicts because I wanted to belong too. Maybe all of my melodramatic, Christian missionizing was really just me trying to fit in, to feel like I belonged. Maybe I was just using my Christianity and my 'call' to just fit in with them? I couldn't shake that feeling.

I said just a few words, as I remember... I recall I had all of the LAM participants stand up. As they were standing I paused again...as I glanced to my right I saw Mark Darnell standing up near the wall: no more than 150 pounds, 52 years old...looking like he was in his early 70's. I hadn't seen Mark in a while but the only thing that had changed was he had gotten some new teeth (his Pit Bull Yetti had chewed up his old ones). He had been in the LAM Program since August of 2015, being in the first group of guys after we reentered the jail after being shut-down for 4 months. He had been in huge legal trouble, getting nabbed in Knox County with a bunch of out-of-county meth from God knows where. I recall offending him greatly (which he reminded me of often) when during his initial interview I had the audacity of guessing that his tired and worn-out look was that of an alcoholic. He quickly corrected me, proudly stating that he was a meth addict and NOT a poor, pathetic alcoholic. I had decided to work with him and work with him and work with him...month after month...After a good period of testing him, I approached the Knox County Prosecutor Dirk Carnahan with the LAM 'stamp of approval.' Amazingly, Dirk worked with me and Mark's attorney Jeff Neal and gave him a wonderful opportunity. Mark was released to the LAM House in the fall of 2016. He ended up staying there with us for about a year, when he was released on probation and he moved out.

Mark's story was filled with abandonment and pain, long prison terms and survival from the early days of the meth surge in Middle America. His father was a cop and Mark had unusual disdain for him. After Mark shared his story of his father's cruelty and abandonment of not only him but also his 8 brothers and 1 sister I understood his anger toward his now deceased father. It was mind-boggling. When I was listening to his story I couldn't believe he had survived this life of his?! Yet there he was, standing up against the far wall of the Community Center, staring up at me as I spoke my last words in this great war. He was the poster-child of the walking wounded, one of the survivors in this crippling war...drinking by age 6, acid and meth by age 9 and high almost every day of his life since the age of 10. He told me once that he only trusted his common sense, "I don't trust no one, not even my family." During that talk back in 2015 he paused and looked at me, "I've been around dope so much it doesn't even register as being illegal...it's a part of my life, it's like breathing."

As I walked off that stage that night I remember how I felt like I was walking out into a sea of family. I went to my seat and I sat down. It felt like home.

J.T.

I'm done with LAM. I have moved on and now serve as the pastor of First Christian Church in Vincennes. The stress level has gone way down and I can truly concentrate on raising my kids and being a good husband. But I miss the guys at the jail. I miss that comradery, that feeling of belonging. I still see some LAM people from time to time; Conrad and William, Talia and Anna and Butch and Willy and Kathy and Steve. Sometimes a guy will be going by my big blue house and walk up and knock on the door and say hey. Sometimes I see them around town and they either avoid me or we chat for a bit.

The other day I was at the nearby Coffee House and I was going to my car after a visit with a friend. I spotted a rough-looking kid walking toward me and I recognized him. It was JT, a kid I hadn't seen in over a year. Actually I hadn't really wanted to see him and I knew he didn't want to see me. He was 21 or 22 years old, something like that...he had been in the jail program for about 9 months. When he was released I had picked him up at the jail and he was so excited and had taken him straight to the LAM House. He was planning big things with his life, you know college and stability and a middle class existence yet he never even made it past curfew that first night (9:30 pm), taking off and leaving all of his stuff in his abandoned room. He had traded stability for absolute chaos.

There he was, walking toward me. He weighed about 100 lbs., his pale face all scratched and red-sored...an old black eye was now green and yellow and his crooked and yellow teeth all matted. He looked exhausted as he put on a smile for me. He might have been high or maybe not (sometimes with meth you can't tell)...but he was definitely scared, telling me a guy was after him. I knew that guy too and he needed to be scared, real scared. Maybe he was twacked-out and paranoid from the meth or the bath salts or the K2 or the lack of sleep for the past 2-3 weeks...who knows. His hands shook as he told me he had some brass knuckles with a blade on one end just in case he met him. He was one of these kids who was not jail material (as they say) so when he talked tough like that it just made you feel sorry for him. He had been in the jail program just to keep from getting his ass kicked all the time by different pod bosses all over the jail. His life was no different on the outside, still just trying to survive, not sure who he could trust.

I offered to buy him some water and a bite to eat. We sat and talked for a bit on the porch of the coffee house as the May skies began to rumble. We were sitting there and he was facing the busy street, his eyes darting back and forth as he ate this chocolate muffin, stuffing his mouth with his dirty fingers. A huge coal train began to rumble by in front of us, its horn blaring so loudly we had to look away from one another. After the train had passed we didn't linger or small talk about the jail program or anything. He was in survival mode. He asked if I could drop him off at the hospital so he could charge his phone. We got in my car and I drove him to Good Samaritan Hospital and pulled up to the ER entrance. He gathered his little backpack and his charging cord. I muttered something to him about keeping in touch or letting me know if I could help but my words faded quickly as he glided out of the car without saying a word.

I drove back home to my house and sat on the front porch of my 1904 three-toned blue Victorian as the Winnipeg-grey sky above my Knox County home opened up with a torrential downpour. I sat and closed my eyes as the spray from the down-pour gently covered my cheeks. For a few moments everything was going to be o.k. For a moment all the dirt and grime and filth were being washed away by the rain.

The 'Sorting-Out'

When I began seminary I had no interest whatsoever in prison or jail ministry. In fact I wasn't a drinker and had only smoked pot one time in my life (and I hated it). I had no business doing the LAM ministry in the first place, but there I was, called to doing it. I was never interested in the criminal justice part of it. I was interested in this ministry because at the time (2005) no one was helping them. There was no specific effort to help the incarcerated drug addict find clean living or sobriety.

For some reason I was fascinated with another class of felons sitting in our county jail: the drug-addict whose disease has taken over their life. This takes some 'sorting-out.' Our program was given the opportunity by our local Sheriff Mike Morris to go within the jail and begin to sort them out, to begin the process of sorting out the good from the bad and give the addicts who are just that, just addicts and NOT criminals, a chance to get out of this downward spiral which ended in damaging and lengthy jail and prison terms.

I loved working in the jail, spending time in the building itself...among the guards, the road officers and the jail staff in the jail, but most of all I cherished spending time with the inmates. Why? Because I got to do this 'sorting out.' I loved being on the 'front-lines' of this essential activity of maintaining our civilized life. Just as much as the officers and law enforcement have a duty to maintain this order in our society, I also believe it is equally important for social workers and ministers to be in the jail itself and sort out the ones who have no business being there, no business. The county jail should be the first line of ministry and work for both churches and social workers, but ironically it is one of the most neglected places within each community.

The jails are populated with so many people who do not belong there and I look at it like this: I got to search for the ones who are really just victims of abuse...layer upon layer of abuse upon abuse, heaped upon them by generation after generation of equally abused relatives and a family of ancestors who never received help either. I found out that many, many drug addicts sitting in the plethora of county jails in this country are really seeking a way out of this death spiral. Their drug abuse is just a way to escape this trauma for just a little while. Drugs are a way of escape. It is not a moral failure. Drug addicts are not weak individuals. On the contrary, drug addicts are some of the most resilient, bravest and toughest people I have ever encountered, bar none. They are survivors...most of them surviving more trauma and abandonment before they reached their teenage years than I ever will in my entire life. If the zombie apocalypse ever happens I know exactly who to call.

Many drug addicts and alcoholics are really seeking a way to re-link with themselves, with their children and mother and father and with their community and with their God. They are really just seeking a way to transcend the limitations of this human life that have trapped them for so long. This is what LAM does: we try to help them escape this trap and help them take flight and soar. 4

Thanks for taking time...

I wrote this book because I need to understand what happened...what happened to the addicts and alcoholics in the program, what happened to our community and also what happened to me? Above all, I have been transformed on a deep level and I need to voice this, I need to try and understand this.

Plain and simple: I love to write. It seems to be my cosmic calling in life. I have always written poetry or short stories or kept a journal...creative writing was my major at IUPUI. I am most comfortable in my skin when I am writing. In the past 10 years I have written several books and I always end up realizing one thing about each project: I am really just asking one central question and it is always centered around my self-understanding...whether it is defining a friendship with a mystic, doing the autopsy on an intense period of suffering, my relationship with the church of my understanding or why a fellow preacher was so cruel to me. I need to know things and the way I discover the answers to these questions is through writing.

This book is my attempt at understanding my relationship with this LAM ministry with people in recovery as it/they have altered the course of my personal and professional life. This book is me attempting to explain these relationships to me: my relationships with my adopted community, my relationship with my God as well as my relationships with these total strangers who have become my friends, my sparring-partners and close confidants and allies.

All I know is this: when you truly invest yourself into real and significant relationship with other human beings and with God's creation, you end up having to sacrifice something of yourself. True ministry and true social work is about self-sacrifice, whether you like it or not.

Within this book you have (hopefully) gotten to know me. Why? Because I have put everything I am into this ministry. Even though at the time of this writing I have moved on from LAM and I am pastoring a church again, I believe LAM will define me and my ministry. It became my life's work, both professionally and personally, yet I had no business founding and directing LAM, since I am not an addict or alcoholic. I am a skinny, floppy-eared, smart-mouthed wanna-be rebel/hippie who grew up with a middle-class life of white-privilege in Southern Indiana as a clean-cut preacher's kid who struggled to follow in his successful Preacher-Dad's footsteps who got the 'call' to Christian ministry. Little did I know that I would not be a pastor of a little county-seat church with two kids and a dog and a nice little pension waiting for me in retirement. My life has taken several twists and turns with personal and professional setbacks (especially when I was in my 20's). Even though I am not a recovering addict or alcoholic I ended up using my background in social work and ministry to start a ministry for addicts and alcoholics. I never thought I would ever do a jail ministry, but I loved it.

This book is for those of you who want a blueprint about how you can create a new community of recovering addicts in your own community, all the while energizing your community in an ecumenical and politics-free, grassroots movement which makes happy both the Liberal and the Libertarian in your community. This book is about the empowering of your community which has been ravaged, baffled and smothered by the drug crisis (in its myriad of forms and cycles). It is about taking back your children, your community and your Country...and it all starts in the local jail. How many 'Brents' are in your community who need a safe place to go? How many?

By sharing our story it is my hope that you can start your own story in your own community. When I started LAM in 2005 we had no blueprint. Our community had to start from scratch. Let the story of LAM be your blueprint. Let the lives of those in our recovery program be your blueprint. Let this book be the place to start.

Notes

Notes on the Introduction

1. Gabriel Glaser's 2013 book entitled "Her Best Kept Secret" is a wonderful exploration of non-12 Step recovery approaches.
2. Jacob Kang-Brown and ram Subramanian. *Out of Sight: The Growth of Jails in Rural America.* New York: Vera Institute of Justice. 2017, 3.
3. Ibid, 6.
4. Ibid, 8-9.
5. Pfaff, John F. "Locked In: The True Causes of Mass Incarceration-And How to Achieve Real Reform." Basic Books, New York. 2017, viii.
6. Ibid, 132.
7. Kurtz, Ernest. "Not-God: A History of Alcoholics Anonymous." Hazeldon. Center City, Minnesota. 1979, 34.

Notes on Part I: Hopelessness

1. I am a huge fan of Herman Melville and poet Charles Olson. Olson's 1947 seminal study of Melville entitled "Call Me Ishmael: A Study of Melville" made a tremendous impact on my life and ministry. It speak eloquently of Olson's take on Melville's interpretation (from 1851, mind you) and analysis of a young America's relationship to space and nature and national identity. This is extremely relevant to our current political condition in

America in 2018, in particular the prevalent struggle with our struggle to find a balanced approach to environmental policies and national security. I invite you to take a look at this deeply spiritual approach to the greatest American novelist, Herman Melville.

2. While I pastored Salem UCC in Westphalia, Indiana from January 2002 until July 2007, I saw firsthand another marginalized group of people in that community: physically and psychologically abused women. I remember one woman in particular who was beaten, brutally beaten by her husband for years and everyone, including her own parents told her to remain faithful and quiet about the subject. When I arrived in Westphalia, she and her husband were still together. I spent a considerable amount of time listening to the stories of her life of survival in this horrific marriage. She had such issues of trauma...all I could do was listen. Shortly before I left Westphalia, she divorced her husband after 50 years of marriage. She passed away several years ago. I was asked to do the funeral of her ex-husband when he passed away, but I kindly declined the offer to be involved in his funeral.

3. Segal, Gerdes and Steiner, 3.

4. Ibid, 3.

5. Ibid, 4-5.

6. Ibid, 5.

7. Ibid, 6.

8. Ibid, 11-26.

9. Out of the approximately 15 male LAM participants on any given day I had three 'team leaders' chosen to help keep order and make the decisions regarding punishments and membership.

10. Gassman, R., Jun,M., Samuel, S., Agley, J.D., King, R., Ables,E., Lee,J., &Wolf, J. (2016) *Indiana Youth Survey-2016.* Bloomington, IN; Indiana Prevention Resource Center.

11. Weisheit, Ralph and White, William. "Methamphetamine: It's History, Pharmacology and Treatment." Hazelden Publishing, Center City, Minnesota, 2009. Pg 26-27.

12. Ibid. Pg. 27.

13. Ibid. Pg. 27.

14. DuPont, Robert L. "The Selfish Brain: Learning From Addiction." Hazelden Publishing, Center City, Minnesota, 2000. Pg. 165.

15. Ohler, Norman. "Blitzed: Drugs in Nazi Germany." Allen Lane (Penguin Books) Great Britain. 2015, 41-42.

16. Kamienski, 110.

17. Encalada, Debbie. "Nazis Were Fueled by Crystal Meth." Complex.com September 14, 2015. 9/16/2015. http://www.complex.com/pop-culture/2015/09/hitler-nazis-were-high-on-meth-records-show

18. Kamienski, 121.

19. Ibid, 121.

20. Weisheit and White. Pg. 30-31.

21. DuPont. Pg. 165.

22. Kamienski, 2.

23. Ibid, 16.

24. Ibid, 19.

25. Ibid, 22.

26. Ibid, 77, 82.

27. Ibid, 146.

28. Ibid, 189.

29. Ibid, 216.

30. Ibid, 209.

31. Ibid, 209.

32. Ibid, 215.

Notes on Part II: Deflation

1. Waldman, Paul. "Six Charts that Explain Why Our Prison System Is So Insane." August 15, 2013. 7-31-15. http://prospect.org/article/six-charts-explain-why-our-prison-system-so-insane

2. Surico, John. "How America Became the Most Imprisoned Nation in the World." October 2, 2015. 10-9-15. http://www.vice.com/read/america-incarcerated-0000765-v22n10

3. Ibid.

4. Waldman, Paul.

5. Ibid.

6. Surico, John. "How America Became the Most Imprisoned Nation in the World." October 2, 2015. 10-9-15. http://www.vice.com/read/america-incarcerated-0000765-v22n10

7. Segal, Gerdes and Steiner, 3.

8. Ibid, 10.

9. Ibid, 320.

10. Ibid, 413.

11. Luke 11:39 in translated in the NIV as "Now then, you Pharisees clean the outside of the cup and dish, but inside you are full of *greed* and wickedness." Nearly all of the translations agree on the word "wickedness" with a few translations using "iniquity" (Douay-Rheims) or "evil" (God's Word, Christian Standard, Good News, Contemporary English, Holman Christian Standard). Yet the word for "greed" is sometimes translated as "plundering" (Berean Literal) or "robbery" (New American Standard) or "ravening" (King James) or "violence" (Good News) or "extortion" (New Heart) or "rapine" (Douay-Rheims) or "plunder" (Darby) or "rape" (Aramaic).

12. Amis, Robin. "A Different Christianity: Early Christian Esotericism and Modern Thought." State University of New York Press, 1995. 9.

13. www.therapeuticjustice.com 5-3-07

14. Kurtz, Ernest. "Not-God: A History of Alcoholics Anonymous." Hazelden Publishing, Center City, Minnesota, 1979. 21.

15. Forsythe, Lance/Hicks, Aretha/Patton, Penny B./ Moss, V. Morgan. "Center For Therapeutic Justice's Community Model: The Jail Administrator's Best Friend-Security Friendly Programming." *American Jails.* January-February 2006. 36.
16. Ibid. 36.
17. Ibid. 37.

Notes on Part III: Conversion

1. McLeod, S. A. (2014). Maslow's Hierarchy of Needs. Retrieved from www.simplypsychology.org/maslow.html

Notes on Epilogue: The grand banquet hall

1. Kamienski, Lukasz. "Shooting Up: A Short History of Drugs and War." Oxford University Press. New York. 2016, 308.
2. Segal, Elizabeth A., Gerdes, Karen E., Steiner, Sue. "An Introduction to the Profession of Social Work: Becoming a Change Agent." Thomson Brooks/Cole Publishing. Belmont,   California. Paper, 419.

About the Author

Peter Denbo Haskins is an ordained clergy in the United Church of Christ. He is the author of several books, including *Mystic in the Graveyard, The Transforming Power of Suffering, God Entered My Life* and *Seeking God in Violent Times* and two books of fiction entitled *Shepherds of the Apocalypse* and *Wolves of the Apocalypse.* He currently serves as the Senior Pastor of First Christian Church (DOC) in historic, colorful downtown Vincennes. A proud, independent native of the Hoosier State, he lives in a blue Victorian in Vincennes, Indiana with his wife Emily and their children Dylan, Catherine and Jack. He can be reached at peterdhaskins@yahoo.com

Made in the USA
San Bernardino, CA
12 December 2019